"Amy has been one of my dearest friends, a relationship that has developed into one of my longest, most loving, and spiritually impactful relationships of my life. She is a soul sister, and I thank God for her every day! You'll love her story, as I do. So sit back and relax—you're in good hands."

—CHRISTEL STURM, longtime friend and accountability partner, Realtor

"Have you ever longed for a friend who 'gets' you? Amy Bridges is that friend you can relate to. Walking through her story, Amy lends her vulnerable heart to true healing by giving you a look inside her authentic self. As I read her story, I saw her grow into the beautiful soul she exhibits today. Let her story inspire and challenge you. She is your friendly guide to help you along the way to your own discovery journey. She holds your hand and knows how you have silently suffered from shame and guilt. Her encouragement will cause you to rise up and be confident in your own identity to emerge a stronger person, the beauty God has created you to be."

—JANELLE KEITH, author coach and editor, Woven Books; author, *Grace For Your Waist: Living a Lifestyle Fitted with Hope*, and *Shaped by Grace: Lose the Lies and Gain God's Truth*.

Another Face in the Crowd

Stop Hiding and Start Living

AMY BRIDGES

This book is dedicated to many:

My parents who have always loved me and siblings
who can understand me.

My husband, who stuck it out with me through
many years of depression and who I now
consider my best friend.

My children, who grew up alongside me, as I
was a late bloomer and still blossoming into
the person I want to be.

Friends, who make life more enjoyable,
and at times, simply survivable.

Mentors, who have impacted and changed
the trajectory of my life.

The girl in myself who was willing to bare it all. You
are courageous and bold. I am proud of you.

But most importantly, to the one who does not believe
in themselves. This book is dedicated to you. It's
dedicated to the good in humanity and a precious
God who created us all.

May you find peace with yourselves and others.
Flourish in the freedom you've been given. Blossom
into the beautiful creation you were born to be. And
impact others with your life story.

Contents

Foreword

Let me introduce you to my friend Amy Bridges. She wants you to know she's your friend too. Through her story of pain, heartache, and struggle, Amy has grown like a wildflower in the wide-open field of God's grace. Through telling her story, she invites you into her inner world of her personal childhood, adulthood, motherhood, and newfound freedom. She leads the way to discovering your true identity and shares the foundations that have paved the way to finding her own.

Have you felt like no one else on the planet could relate to the type of thoughts you have about yourself or others? Not just in relation to your physical circumstances and daily life—but in the dark recesses of your own mind? Do you feel like you're a passenger on the crazy train, trying desperately to keep that engine on the circular track that only loops in your own head? What if you opened up to someone and all that hysterical panic and dreary pessimism came steamrolling right out? Furthermore, there's terror of exposing how needy and shame filled you are, mixed with arrogance and self-judgment.

If you tend to suffer in silence, like so many of us sadly do, the fear of being found weak, weird, or worthless just seems too high a risk. Author Amy Bridges had silently suffered for way too long. So she has walked in those same shoes. She learned those worn-out shoes will eventually rub blisters on your spiritual feet and leave your heart wounded. When she realized she was wallowing in her pain, feeling alone and emotionally worn, she pledged to do something about it. She learned how to fight for what was important.

Get to know Amy's heart and let her help you through her story. It is written from a friendly point of view from a heart of love. Amy gives a fresh perspective on an age-old identity problem and shares how she walked her journey to gain more freedom, wisdom, and understanding. This relatable pursuit of *Who am I?* and *Why am I like this?* and *Will I ever belong?* are experienced through the hardships, the hope, and the ongoing healing she has found in this flawed world.

Amy offers a powerful tool we all possess—a personal testimony to help another along. Amy leads the way, giving you a helping hand out of your depression and anxiety. She lifts the invisible veil of her heart to say, "You are not alone, your life matters, and I have been there TOO!" This book fearlessly reveals her most cherished and hidden places. You will be drawn into the beauty of her soul as she unearths the buried bones of lies that continuously cry out to be resurrected. Inside her memories and God-guided life lessons, you'll find the bond of sameness and unity, in addition to your own uniqueness and favor.

Be encouraged through her openness about her own shortcomings. Amy never gave up on the long, winding road to find forgiveness as she journeyed into the unknown. Her unending desire to grow, while retaining a teachable spirit, is remarkable and showed her tremendous capacity to love.

Amy will cheer you on from the sidelines and challenge you to seek out the Lord in your struggles. As you wait on the Lord's rescue, you will also learn to fight fiercely for what matters most to you. Most important, you'll learn that giving up is not an option.

Her gentle spirit helps you bring awareness to your own short-comings and tenderly leads you to a path of healing. Her prayer is for you to find a sense of your self-worth, reigning peace, consuming joy, and above all, a clearer understanding of Jesus Christ as Lord and Savior and your personal Friend.

Through Amy's story, you will feel the love, comfort, and understanding seep into your heart as you read each word. Her vulnerability will break down the walls to let in God's peace, comfort, and most important, rest to your own overworked mind. I hope through the Lord's anointing power, you will relate to these life lessons yourself as if she is sitting next to you in your living room. Her testimony of God's healing grace will free your spirit and dispel the cloud of stress and anxiety by the essence of her very presence.

Friend, life may tell you that you are just another face in the crowd. But you are about to embark on a spiritual trek that will build your understanding of who you are in Christ and rid you of misunderstood thoughts, anxiety-ridden fears, the need for approval, and your desire for position. Best of all, God's love will shine through. God wants you to know you are never lost in a crowd. He knows you by name, He sees you, His thoughts are for you, and YOU are precious in His sight.

For this reason I kneel before the Father, from whom every family in heaven and on earth derives its name. I pray that out of his glorious riches he may strengthen you with power through his Spirit in your inner being, so that Christ may dwell in your hearts through faith. And I pray that you, being rooted and established in love, may have power, together with all the Lord's holy people, to grasp how wide and long and high and deep is the love of Christ, and to know this love that surpasses knowledge—that you may be filled to the measure of all the fullness of God. Now to him who is able to do immeasurably more than all we ask or imagine, according to his power that is at work within us, to him be glory in the church and in Christ Jesus throughout all generations, for ever and ever! Amen.

(Ephesians 3:14-21 NIV)

Christel Sturm

one

Longing for Labels

For he satisfies the longing soul, and the
hungry soul he fills with good things.
(Psalm 107:9)

Have you noticed the human race as a whole longs for labels? From a young age, influenced by the world around us, we are conditioned to believe we need labels to define our being. As children, it's ballerinas and baseball players. Moving into adolescence, the labels shift to new aspirations like cheer captain, quarterback, and valedictorian. In adulthood, we strive to climb the ladder of success or seek out opportunities that will give our lives meaning and purpose.

Growing up, I accepted so many negative labels as truth and let them define me, only to arrive at a place in life that lacked fulfillment. Every failed attempt to define myself with a desired label led me deeper into depression. My insecurities became so prevalent that I couldn't decipher between them and my true self. This fueled my anxiety and internalized anger. I was an emotional roller coaster. My confidence plummeted as fear took over, consuming me with depression.

I wrestled in my own strength throughout the years to scratch my way out of a body that seemed foreign to me. Even some of my closest friends didn't know the gravity of the self-deprecating dialogue in my mind. During these seasons, I often felt alone in the darkness of my thoughts. Misunderstood and crazy. I feared ridicule and judgment of everyone's perceived thoughts, which caused me to quickly isolate myself and go into hiding.

I bought into the lie that I was shy. I began excusing myself from conversations, telling myself it was because I was an introvert. Because I would get overwhelmed and easily angered, I thought it best to remove myself from the equation for everyone's safety. The truth is I'm not really a shy person. I came across that way when fear kept me from being my authentic self. Once fear had set in, the awkwardness in crowds intensified. To be seen as the real me was scary. Transparency was intimidating, and fear of looking ridiculous or stupid was paralyzing.

Honestly, I didn't talk much because I didn't feel like I had anything worth saying. I felt like a dumb girl who got left behind, suffering on the growth charts of life. I desired so badly to be free from the bondage that lies kept me in, but fear still had its grip on me. Exhausted with life and desperate, I knew something had to change. I couldn't sustain life in this unhealthy cycle any longer. I knew it would be impossible on my own, so I reached out for help through counseling.

During the times with my counselor, she reminded me that at some time or another, our actions themselves are not the problem but merely symptoms of something much more substantial. This idea is not solely limited to drug and alcohol abuse but can also be connected to destructive thought patterns and negative belief systems. With this newfound understanding, I realized it was going to take a willingness on my part to allow God to fully examine my heart. It would demand hard work to uncover the deep internal root of my struggle. On the precipice, I anticipated there would be pain ahead. But I knew I must press on.

On my own, my thoughts had not gone to the depths of discovery I was learning through counseling. Instead, I figured my problems were due to a personality defect. Somewhere along the way, I conditioned myself to find coping mechanisms to treat the symptoms rather than dealing with the deeply rooted wounds that caused all the turmoil inside my soul.

THE QUESTION THAT KICK-STARTED IT ALL

The Holy Spirit began revealing lies I was believing, and my soul thirsted for more truth. I began welcoming God into the conversation and asked, "God, where did all this start?" I prayerfully sifted through the memories from my past. What label was I really after? It was the esteemed label of being *normal* I coveted. Something within me was hurting and needed approval, complete with accolades, to cover the shame I felt. That desire to be an important *somebody* has followed me around for years.

Coming from divorced parents, our family had its struggles. My mom raised us for the most part while our dad took out-of-town jobs and saw us when he could. Our family struggled physically and financially on a regular basis. I began comparing myself and my family to others early on. My family dynamic was loud and argumentative, and it thrived on drama. I longed for the polar opposite. Growing up, I prided myself in being the peacemaker. However, I've realized that I learned from an early age to be a *peacekeeper.* If I could hide in the shadows and not rock the boat, everything would be fine. If I could be sugary sweet and nice, I would be accepted. I overcorrected in fear of coming off too strong and forceful—and somehow suppressed the fighter within me.

THE HEART OF THE MATTER

I wanted to be somebody else from as far back as I can remember. In school, my all-time favorite movie was *Pretty Woman*. I watched it so many times I could recite every word. Any girl who grew up in the 1980s and '90s knows exactly what I'm talking about. I longed to be Julia Roberts's character, Vivian, with her smile and insatiable laugh. I wanted to stroll down the sidewalks of Rodeo Drive, window-shopping and daring to venture into the fancy, upscale boutiques. It's thrilling to dream of, isn't it? A modern-day Cinderella story. Let's not forget every awkward young girl's dream to be Jennifer Grey in *Dirty Dancing*, winning the hunk and dancing the night away. I have always rooted for the underdog—because in every life event, that's what I felt I was. I don't believe I am alone in this desire to rise above the limits we have placed on ourselves.

For you created my inmost being; you knit me together in my mother's womb. I praise you because I am fearfully and wonderfully made; your works are wonderful, I know that full well.
(Psalm 139:13-14)

Before we are born, unique gifts and talents are knitted within us, but because of our humanness and the sin we are born into, our gifts can easily be twisted into selfish desires. You may not describe it quite like I do, but I would be willing to bet you struggle or have struggled with similar feelings. We long to be important, for our life to matter, to somehow impact others with our existence. Somewhere deep down, we believe the only way that will happen is if our name is in the rolling credits, stretched across a billboard, or in flashing lights. I'm here to tell you—that is an absolute lie.

Let's go back, not to the '80s but a little further. Lights, camera, action! Scene 1 in the Garden of Eden. After God created man, he gave him authority over all the earth with one exception.

And the Lord God commanded the man, "You are free to eat from any tree in the garden; but you must not eat from the tree of knowledge of good and evil, for when you eat of it you will surely die."
(Genesis 2:16-17)

I read a note about this section of scripture that stood out to me: "God's command was given to Adam as a moral test. It placed before him a conscious, deliberate choice to believe and obey or to disbelieve and disobey his Creator's will." God created us in His image. But that wasn't good enough for Eve, and from experience, it hasn't been for me either. I wanted it all! Even though God gave humanity free rule and reign over all the earth and all the creatures, Eve was still tempted not to just be like God but to *be* God. She didn't want to surrender to God's authority; she wanted complete control.

When we strive for recognition and do not acquire it, we are vulnerable to becoming bitter if we allow our focus to be on ourselves instead of God. This is why it is so important to know God and His Word, so that we are not deceived by lies. So what are you looking for? Are you looking for a label of authority and influence over others? Is it to look smart? To stand out in a crowd? I know for me, I constantly revolved through different labels I desired..

I wanted to honor God with my life, but honestly, at the time, I think I desired honor for myself more. I wanted so badly to break away from the negative labels I had placed on myself and my family. I remember a woman talking about me to my fiancé. She said, "The apple doesn't fall far from the tree." That was such a hurtful comment that stung deeply and has stuck with me over the years. My parents weren't perfect, and yes, they did end up divorcing, facing opposition. As a result, we struggled mentally, physically, emotionally, and financially. I wish someone would have spoken the truth to that woman: that our words either speak life or they speak death. Heck, I guess I wish I had known that for myself back then too.

MISPLACED ANGER

I saw my parents struggle with pain first hand, and I judged them for what they put our family through. As an immature teenager, I didn't have compassion for them but instead blamed them for all my problems. Have you ever struggled with the need to place the blame on someone else because you don't want to be held accountable? I wanted people to think highly of me, and I kept blaming other people so I wouldn't have to look at myself. But how could I ever be different if I didn't forgive? Yes, the mistakes and sins of others affect our lives. But we cannot allow them to be an excuse for our bitterness or allow lies to dominate our behavior—because our sins and mistakes affect others as well.

When I found myself pregnant at eighteen, I questioned, "God, what have I gotten myself into?" How had I fallen into the stereotypical group of teen pregnancies I worked so hard to avoid? This was not who I wanted to be. These were not the labels I desired for myself, but a compilation of poor decisions led me there. The enemy works best with tiny slivers of truth, mixed with his multitude of lies, to take many of us down. And he was doing a really good job at discouraging me.

As time went by, my youthful face and growing belly drew attention and were impossible to hide. By that time, I had already heard one too many times, "You're having a baby? You're just a baby yourself." I felt defeated, exposed in my sin and shame. I tried to ignore the embarrassment and focus on my newfound titles of soon-to-be mom and wife. Those labels filled me in a way I can't explain. They made my life feel important and purposeful.

THE ULTIMATE LABEL

What labels do you covet, and when you get them, do they satisfy? Is it the college degree, the government badge, the gold nameplate on the door? Do they make you special? Do they fulfill you? Sure, they suffice for a little while. But if we are anything like some of the men in the Bible, then I'm sure not for very long. For instance, take James and John. If you're not familiar with them, let me explain who they are. James and John were brothers, some of the very first men appointed to be Jesus's disciples. Remember the famous words of Jesus: *Come follow me and I will make you fishers of men?* (Matthew 4:19 NIV) He then called them as His disciples. Not only so, but they were chosen from the twelve disciples to be included in Jesus's smaller, more intimate circle, along with Peter. You'd think those labels would be enough, wouldn't you? Right next to Jesus in the ultimate *inner circle*. They weren't though. Mark 10:35-45 references this story. *It's good.* Go read it for yourself! Read below what James and John asked Jesus.

Let one of us sit at your right and the other at your left in your glory.
(Mark 10:37)

When the other disciples heard this, they were indignant. Angered, outraged, and annoyed by the suggested unfair treatment. They weren't so appalled by the request in itself as to the unfairness of someone being greater than them. OUCH! I know, right? What is it inside of us that has to rear its ugly head and be at the top? Nobody wants to believe they struggle with pride, jealousy, or envy, but that's certainly what it is. If you've noticed this kind of response from yourself, it's a good time to have a heart check.

> Jesus called them together and said, "You know that those who are regarded as rulers of the Gentiles lord it over them, and their high officials exercise authority over them. Not so with you. Instead, whoever wants to become great among you must be your servant, and whoever wants to be first must be slave of all. For even the Son of Man did not come to be served, but to serve, and to give his life as a ransom for many."
> (Mark 10:42-45)

Also, the timing of James and John's request made it even worse. Jesus had just had a moment of vulnerability, telling His closest friends and associates about His looming death sentence. They totally missed the pain and suffering Jesus would endure but wanted all the reward of joining in the resurrection and glory. *Isn't that just like a human to avoid any or all of the suffering and hard work but expect all the reward in return?*

If we continue seeking worldly labels, even though they seem to satisfy for a little while, we will be sorely disappointed. Do not be deceived. God is the only one who can quench our thirsty souls for position, which makes sense because He created within us a void only He can fill.

I actually want to challenge the idea that the world conditions us for labels. Because before the world existed as we know it, the Bible says:

> Then God said, "Let us make human beings in our image, to be like us. They will reign over the fish in the sea, the birds in the sky, the livestock, all the wild animals on the earth, and the small animals that scurry along the ground."
> (Genesis 1:26 NLT)

Since the beginning of time, we were made to be like Christ. We are His image bearers. May I venture to say it is not simply a label that can be removed but it was weaved into our DNA by God himself. It is who you and I were created to be; it is the purpose for which we are on the earth. It's not a label that allows us to be puffed up about ourselves. This DNA wasn't put inside of us to highlight our own names but to highlight His. God, in His love for us, has given us a label, but we don't allow God to be king in our lives. Instead of being set apart for God, we want to be like the rest of the world, having kings or labels to rule over us. Just as a work of art reflects the artist himself, God's image is reflected through us—that is, if we choose to align with His will. Unlike artwork, we are living, breathing humans gifted with a free will. Our wonderful God is not a dictator that forces us to love Him. He is a loving God that gives us the freedom of choice.

"Where we are is not who we are." This is a calming quote from one of the many counselors/mentors I have had in my healing journey. Breathe that in for a moment. The ugliness inside that I am pointing out is not meant to shame. It is an opportunity for light to be shed in the darkness of our hearts. This does not mean we are "bad" people, but it does mean that we are misaligned with the truth. If you have been in agreement with dark destructive lies that interfere with relationships and true happiness, this is the book for you. This is the time for you. As I share my story of healing, this is me walking with you through yours. There is hope. You are not alone. I am cheering you on!

What labels do you currently desire for yourself? What is the motivation behind these labels? Take your time and be as honest as you can.

____

____

____

In what situations have you compared yourself to others or been envious? Name as many as you can.

____

____

____

Are you willing to allow God to examine your heart? Calling out each situation above, ask God to forgive you and cleanse you from these experiences and the negativity you've held inside. Take a deep breath in and, as you breathe out, visualize the weight being lifted.

____

____

____

Your Life Matters...

HEALING IS ON THE HORIZON. I have created space for you to journal what stands out to you through your story. Please don't skip this step, as I believe it is where we release things we didn't even know we were holding on to. Write something—anything. Healing is coming!

SONG INSPIRATION
"You Say" by Lauren Daigle; "Reckless Love" by Cory Asbury

two

Don't Like What You See?

The Lord is close to the brokenhearted and

saves those who are crushed in spirit.

(Psalm 34:18)

gladly stepped into the role of being a wife. I had always dreamed of being a mom and envisioned how wonderful it was going to be. Everything was done by the book to ensure the health and safety of my little one. Part of that was eliminating alcohol, cigarettes, even caffeine and adding many fruits and vegetables to my diet. As my belly grew, I was in awe at every movement the baby made and cherished the miracle of it all.

Labor pains came early, around 5:00 a.m. I was awakened by the sharp pangs of my belly tensing into a solid rock. I knew it was baby time. Arriving at the nurse's station on the labor and delivery floor, I told the nurse I thought I was in labor.

She chuckled and explained to both of us, as she was leaving to prepare the exam room, "We will check you, but Daddy, she's still smiling . . . so you're probably going to have to take her to eat."

I was eighteen and pregnant, and her laughter struck a nerve with me. I was afraid she thought I was young and silly. Thankfully, when she checked me, I was dilated to a six, and everyone calmly began moving at a much quicker pace. Within a few hours, I had delivered our son into the world.

Overnight, I had changed from a child myself to having our first child. I had no idea what I was doing but was too proud to admit it. Even though this was all new, I was good at soothing, caring for, and loving my newborn baby boy. During the first couple weeks, we stayed with our grandmother. Everything was great, but I was ready to embrace this journey on our own.

Once we were home, everything began closing in on me. I was a girl on the verge of becoming a *real* woman. I desperately juggled the demands of marriage and motherhood. Loads of laundry and a sink full of dishes equaled failure to me. If I couldn't even tackle motherhood, how was I ever going to be *somebody* or get anywhere in life? Was that the truth? No, but I perceived it to be true. Don't get me wrong, becoming a wife and mother has been the greatest gift besides Jesus himself. The struggle, however, was real.

It's never as simple as learning new things and applying them, like cooking, cleaning, and paying bills. The turmoil inside was much more consequential, deeper than a daily routine. The standard I held of myself to, as I strove to meet the needs of my husband and child, was taking its toll on me. I was definitely my own worst critic and felt disapproval from every direction, which multiplied my insecurities.

My husband purchased a business right before we got married and was overwhelmed by the demands of life as well, torn between family, work, and a social life. For the first year of motherhood, I was alone with our child in the confines of the four walls of our mobile home. In the meantime, I got invited to a few Mary Kay parties and enjoyed the outside adult interaction. I finally had reason to get dressed and put on makeup. I felt valuable again. The idea of it provided me with a glimpse of something to be desired—*opportunity*. I had a deep need to be more than I was and wanted to be like these women.

Meek and naive, not knowing anything about business, sales, or even makeup (really), I crumbled under the beautifully important women. I now held the title of Mary Kay beauty consultant with my very own badge of validation. However, I was terrible at sales. I didn't consider the fact that to be able to sell something, you have to believe in it. There was my problem. I didn't believe I was worth investing in, so I figured if anyone gave me their time, essentially I owed *them*. This attitude resulted in practically giving products away, which raised the volume of my inner critic.

On one particular day, I played dress-up. My inner slogan became *Fake it until you make it*. I made sure my makeup was flawless and packed a kit full of Mary Kay products famously known for producing pink Cadillacs. Sitting at the client's kitchen table, a couple of minutes turned into hours of deep conversation. Our eyes filled to the brim with tears of heartache, of not measuring up, and trying to be people we weren't. There was no resisting this release. Like any good thunderstorm, it washed away some of the grimy buildup in our hearts.

After we shared vulnerability, I knew we'd be lifelong friends. We enjoyed long talks on the phone and spent hours of time together, laughing and avoiding responsibility, only then to have to make up for lost time. We took turns cleaning each other's houses when one was too emotionally fixated on the mess to function. We weren't usually overwhelmed at the same time, so it worked out well. Having a friend was super fun, and this new relationship gave me a fresh hope. She has graciously shown love and given gentle correction, direction, and guidance throughout the years. She's the friend who makes you do cartwheels in your front yard until you can laugh through the tears. Friends you haven't talked to in forever but are able to pick right back up where you left off, never missing a beat, are truly a blessing from God.

A joyful, cheerful heart brings healing to both body and soul. But the one whose heart is crushed struggles with sickness and depression.
(Proverbs 17:22 TPT)

TABLE FOR FOUR

Having a friend helped relieve a sense of loneliness and lowered the expectation I had on my husband to meet my emotional needs. My new friend filled a void I didn't know I had. My spirit was being refreshed and lifted. My relationship with my husband was on the mend. Shortly after, we decided to have another baby; this time, it was a precious little girl. I continued to be a stay-at-home mom, and while I loved the opportunity, I still felt inferior and tempted by the pursuit of something more worthy of recognition. However, I was never able to find the perfect job with perfect hours that would allow me to have both. So I busied myself with motherhood. When it came to loving my children, I was a natural. But that's when pride crept in, and inherently I told God through my actions, *I got this one.* Boy, was I ever wrong!

My only friend's schedule changed when she got a job, and everyone else was in college living totally different lives than me. I was alone for hours on end, running from one child's needs to the other, but that didn't bother me. Honestly, I was right where I wanted to be, even though I still felt stuck. Not seeing another adult for the better part of the day or holding an educated conversation is what was wreaking havoc on my sanity.

Looking back, the bad days weren't so bad. I continued to be disappointed in myself, but it was because I had a skewed view of things. Did it really matter to God in the big scheme if I'd forgotten to brush my hair that day? Who am I kidding—I didn't brush my teeth half of the time until my husband was on his way home from work. Anyway, I had a tendency to focus on the negative even when there were many reasons to be grateful. I couldn't shake the feeling that I wasn't enough, and I struggled with shame and guilt.

Instead of considering myself *just* a stay-at-home mom, I wish I would have realized then what I know to be true now. I was personally investing time, love, energy, and valuable lessons into the relationships God had entrusted to me. What a gift—the ability to speak life into your children. To nurture, teach, and witness all the firsts in their lives. I saw every facial expression, and when they fell, I was there to pick them up and give them security and comfort.

Another blessing I was unaware of at the time was the opportunity to affirm my husband's value and supply him a place of rest. Every day, he would go to the grind to figure out how to provide for our family. He was under pressure and stress of navigating uncharted territories himself. *But sometimes we are so caught up in how hard things are for us that we miss seeing the struggles and pain of those around us.*

Because I didn't have this wisdom then, I was torn between two lifestyles. I felt like I was two different people caught between being a loving, caring, devoted mom and housewife during the day and at night needing communication and connection. My husband came home from work exhausted, needing a quiet place of escape. We were both exhausted in different ways, he from all the interaction and I from the lack of adult interaction. In a marriage without emotional connection, bearing the weight of the parental responsibilities myself,

I resented my husband and removed my heart from the equation so it couldn't be further damaged.

BEAUTY FROM ASHES

Coming from a broken family, I was bound and determined our marriage would survive. But all I knew was to run. Fight or flight, right? The pendulum would swing between the two. We fought something crazy. With everything in me, I wanted to run away but also desperately wanted to make it work, especially for our children. I convinced myself I was worthless and unable to contribute to the world around me. I was blind to my personal values.

Thoughts of being dumb and uneducated would go to war against the cherished dreams of being a family. Would I be barefoot and pregnant forever? I believed the lies I would tell myself. I felt invisible, unwanted, and trapped. And to make matters worse, my husband was right there trapped with me. I felt like a heavy weight to him, like the old ball and chain. These are a mere taste of the circling lies that would breed fury in my mind.

Since I didn't work outside the home, I became the babysitter for others while they spread their wings and soared. If you haven't noticed, I allowed pain, suffering, and bitterness to take root. I didn't see that I was envious of their perceived freedom. I didn't comprehend that people trusted me with caring for their children. Instead, I felt devalued. In reality, I was chosen by the parents and God to love and care for their children. I was trusted to keep them safe and offered the parents peace of mind while they were away.

Isn't it staggering how your mind can conjure contradicting thoughts and somehow believe both to be true? Nonetheless, I didn't like where my life was headed. Because of my situation, I felt obligated to cater to everyone's requests. I didn't have a grip on life; it was out of control. Unraveled and unhinged, I was scrambling to prove something. I pretended and put on a smile even though I didn't know who I was, what I was doing, or where I was going. I lost all hope for my dreams for the future.

NOT WHAT I SIGNED UP FOR

I believed God was punishing me. I made too many poor choices, squandering any hope for myself. These were the consequences of my sin, my lot in life. Fights in our marriage escalated. Not because we didn't love each other but we were both young and selfish, small-minded and broken. We were kids navigating the real world of adulthood. We were not a team. I thought if he won, I lost. We couldn't even talk without throwing insults. We wouldn't listen to each other because we were too busy defending ourselves. We both armored up for the fight.

Walls were built. I felt unseen by my husband and was lost within myself to even know who I was. I saw myself as an obligation and burden to him. I didn't feel special anymore, and the work that mattered seemed exhausting and pointless.

Dark days loomed ahead, running together as if there were no beginning or end. Deprived of intimacy, I believed my only role as a wife was to please my husband physically. The lack of connection was despairing, bringing feelings of dirtiness into our marriage bed.

MY MISERY CONTINUED

Being numb was the most horrible feeling. The substance of my life dissolved into simply existing in *his* world. Unable to make a single decision on the chance of being wrong I disappeared into him until I no longer recognized myself. In my weakness, I gave fear the power to control me. I sank deeper into an unexplainable depression.

Many poor choices were made over the next year, bringing us both to our breaking point. I had threatened to leave before and felt justified in doing so. But this time, it was my husband packing his bags, leaving me and suggesting joint custody. I felt confused and abandoned. How would I survive DIVORCE? Joint custody? My children were everything to me. And really, maybe more than anything, I needed to know my husband loved me. I was overwhelmed and devastated. The emotions came on strong and flooded my body like a tsunami. Continuous waves of anger, guilt, and shame violently crashed over me.

The tragedy of a perfect storm equaled an unrecognizable life. Drained physically, spiritually, and mentally, I held distorted perspectives about our relationship coupled with resentment and bitterness. I needed to know I mattered to my husband even though I thought life would be easier without him. I wanted him to rescue me like Richard Gere did for Julia Roberts in *Pretty Woman*. I wanted the perfect fairytale. What I didn't know was God already had a redeeming plan in action. He was in the process of rescuing both of us.

BUT GOD . . .

Thankfully, God is patient even when we turn away from Him. Sometimes, it takes tripping and falling flat on our faces to get to the point of surrender, but He's faithful to help us back up on our feet. He patiently waits. He saw me and was present when I finally cried out to Him. Completely empty, I had nothing to offer. It's the ideal condition for God's intervention. I confessed and released my raw emotions to Him, alone in the silence, except for the hum of the refrigerator. It reiterated just how alone I felt. I remember that moment so clearly, even though everything else is foggy. I hadn't prayed in years. I didn't know what to pray or even what I wanted, but I knew—in my being—I needed Him. Jesus was the only hope for my future.

I kneeled down beside my bed in the dark room, falling into a somber position of reverence. Groans began to wail from inside as I puddled on the floor in a fetal position. I don't recall any clear words coming out, but He saw me and heard my desperate, genuine, and heartfelt prayer of surrender. This was a literal representation of the following scripture.

And the Holy Spirit helps us in our weakness. For example, we don't know what God wants us to pray for. But the Holy Spirit prays for us with groanings that cannot be expressed with words. And the Father who knows all hearts knows that the Spirit pleads for us believers in harmony with God's own will.

(Romans 8:26-27 NLT)

It was time to choose a life for myself, so I put on my big-girl pants and grabbed hold of God's hand. "Let's do this, God. You lead, and I will follow." The small, intricate moments of surrender are the turning points of a life forever changed.

Thankfully, my husband returned, and we both willingly forgave each other's mistakes and honored the covenant we made. Throughout our marriage, my husband has offered me so much grace, as I have him. Our years of marriage haven't always been a bed of roses, or maybe they have—with the thorny stems and all. My husband continuously reminded me, the grass is not always greener on the other side. The possibility of a life without problems, issues, and drama was so incredibly tempting to me but not realistic. I was searching for perfection. This is another deception from the enemy. I felt like the way author Stephen Covey, in his book *How to Develop Your Personal Mission Statement*, explained it:

"Think about taking a trip on an airplane. Before taking off, the pilot has a very clear destination in mind, which hopefully coincides with yours, and a flight plan to get there. The plane takes off at the appointed hour toward that predetermined destination. But in fact, the plane is off course at least 90 percent of the time. Weather conditions, turbulence, and other factors cause it to get off track. However, feedback is given to the pilot constantly, who then makes course corrections and keeps coming back to the exact flight plan, bringing the plane back on course. And often, the plane arrives at the destination on time. It's amazing. Think of it. Leaving on time, arriving on time, but off course 90 percent of the time. It is the picture of where you want to end up—that is, your destination is the values you want to live your life by. Even if you are off course much or most of the time but still hang on to your sense of hope and your vision, you will eventually arrive at your destination. You will arrive at your destination and usually on time. That's the whole point—we just get back on course."

I had an expectation of what marriage was supposed to be. I grew up watching Cinderella stories just like you and didn't know how to distinguish reality from fairy tales. God promises us: *Here on earth you will have many trials and sorrows. But take heart, because I have overcome the world.* (John 16:33b) It makes sense that two broken people coming from a long lineage of brokenness are going to have troubles. But that doesn't mean we have to compromise our morals. One thing I do know is that prayer and working on yourself goes a long way. From a woman who's been married twenty-three years and counting, I can't express enough that your marriage is worth fighting for. *You* are worth fighting for and so is your spouse.

Over the many years of our marriage, I begged my husband to go to counseling with me. Eventually, he came around to the idea. Slowly but surely, we began working on our communication skills and are still working on them to this very day. Has anyone ever told you that marriage is hard? If not, let me be the first. *Marriage is hard.* Sometimes you might feel nauseated from all the twists and turns on the roller-coaster ride of marriage. But please, don't give up.

Disclaimer: If you are a victim of physical, mental, or emotional abuse in your relationship, please seek professional help.

After my life-altering prayer of surrender, I chose a life for myself—whether anyone was joining me or not. I needed good godly counsel to navigate through our marriage relationship. I soon began bringing our children to church as well. It was a healthy step I had to take for our family. It was one small decision that made a big difference. There comes a time in every life when you are at a crossroads, faced with a pivotal decision. What will you choose?

GOD IS IN EVERY BEND

When I think back to these years, it reminds me of how wonderfully loving God is. How intimate, personal, and willing He is to go to any length to reach us. He sees our broken hearts and fights for us. He rescues us. He brings people into our lives through cherished relationships to encourage us and keep us moving forward. He becomes more than a Savior. He is our close friend we can relate to or a mentor to remind us we are not alone. Is it possible He's doing that for you right now through this book?

If you relate with my story, you may be fighting back tears. Go ahead, let them flow—it's cleansing for the soul. You are seen by the God of all creation. He will continue to send confirmations of His love, acceptance, and desire for you to fully be His. He will never give up on you. It's not in His nature. I'm so grateful for the Christ-centered friendships He brought to my journey; He allowed us to sharpen one another. I'm praying over you right now that God would bring *your people* into your life—that He would give you the gift of friendship and laughter. The gift of a shoulder to cry on. And the gift of His comforting presence.

As iron sharpens iron, so one person sharpens another.
(Proverbs 27:17)

Have you ever found yourself feeling like the walls of life were closing in on you? Explain.

____

____

____

If so, has it been difficult for you to be vulnerable and transparent with someone about your struggle or possible depression?

____

____

____

Please look up the following scriptures, write them out, and speak these verses over your life.

Job 12:22

____

____

____

John 12:46

____

____

____

John 1:5

____

____

____

Psalm 18:28

____

____

____

Psalm 51:1-2, 10

____

____

____

____

____

If you have never accepted Christ as your Savior, or would like to today, add the following scripture.

Read Romans 10:8-13. Write out 10:9

JOURNAL
Your Life Matters...

HEALING IS ON THE HORIZON. I have created space for you to journal what stands out to you through your story. Please don't skip this step, as I believe it is where we release things we didn't even know we were holding on to. Write something—anything. Healing is coming!

SONG INSPIRATION
"Defender" by Rita Springer; "Rebel Heart" by Lauren Daigle; "The Bend in the Road" poem by Helen Steiner Rice

three

Perfection vs. Perfect Son

Looking unto Jesus the author and finisher of our faith;

who for the joy that was set before him endured the cross, despising the

shame, and is set down at the right hand of the throne of God.

(Hebrews 12:2)

God was faithfully aligning many situations in my life. I could see Him everywhere and in everything. He brought people into my life to encourage, bring hope, and instill strength in me. During that time, I was given a book to read that was instrumental in my relationship with the Lord—*The Purpose Driven Life* by Rick Warren. In fact, I would later bribe my children to read it! That book gave me the confidence to begin reading the Bible. I learned how to study my Bible and would get lost in the Word. It was so fulfilling and satisfying—like water to a thirsty soul. I kept going back for more each day, expectant of what He would teach me. In God's faithfulness and love, He always showed up. I couldn't get enough. It was the most beautiful love story of my life. I was free. The weight of the world was behind me, and I was on a new path. This decision brought me freedom and restored my faith. It was one thing that had a profound effect on my whole being.

Unfortunately, as life carried on, I gradually turned away from my divine GPS . . . again. I faced the journey of getting my life together like a to-do list, checking all the boxes. I exchanged the weight of the world for a religious straitjacket, and I bought one in every color for everybody I knew. It was the new style I sported. I think many new Christians have made this mistake. We give God the reins then we quickly take them back. I was the most polished, buttoned-up version of myself I could possibly be. I cleaned up my act and vowed I wasn't going to smoke, drink, or cuss out loud (most of the time). Isn't that what I was supposed to do? I was a new creation and needed to physically appear different as well, right? I was the most patient mother on the outside, but my inner thoughts were still in distress. People would commend me and give accolades for how "together" I was. The praise felt good, but I felt like a fraud.

Joining Bible studies, I learned new revelations but *labored* to apply them *perfectly*. Thank goodness for God's unending grace, because I continued down this "works mentality" road for a while. I was putting all my energy into becoming *perfect*. I dove into cooking extravagant meals for my family, and they loved them. I was a little better at keeping house (I'm not going to lie—this one never really stuck). I would kiss my husband when he got home from work and do his laundry. Planners and organizers were paving the way to the top! My circumstances were improving, and I was getting a better response from others. I had a new lease on life, and this time I wasn't going to screw it up. Isn't it peculiar how the pendulum swings? A few short months prior, I considered myself nothing to see. Yet somehow, I now saw myself as somebody everyone else should follow.

Judgment of others became the self-righteous undertone in my voice. I knew I wasn't better than others but still believed I was better in some regard. I had accepted God's grace for myself because I needed it so gravely but was impatient with others. It's painfully twisted, I know. I wanted to be better than my past and was trying to prove it to everyone around me. My mentor and writing coach described it well: "The wrestling of finding our true self is challenging. It's an endless train track we, as humans, tend to hop on and off throughout difficult times in life."

I didn't understand true sanctification had nothing to do with how good I could be in my own strength or my worst mistakes. But it has everything to do with the redeeming price Jesus paid on the cross. If you are a new Christian, here's a good scripture to meditate on.

Blind Pharisee! First clean the inside of the cup and dish, and then the outside will also be clean.

(Matthew 23:26)

When we clean up our act from the outside in, our heart is not yet clean. God's Word says to clean the inside first and the outside will be clean. In our ignorance or religious misconceptions, we miss the mark. But God doesn't just turn away from us there and say *we'll never learn*—just like we don't do that with our children. I was certainly growing, but I still had a lot to learn for sure.

IN THE DARK

The battle for perfection always results in distress. I wanted to live life perfectly so badly I could taste it. But unsuccessful efforts at perfection were exhausting, and the high I was on came to a crashing halt. Have you ever heard the saying "What we behold, we become"? I became a perfectionist. According to *Merriam-Webster*, *perfectionism* is defined as:

1. a: the doctrine that the perfection of moral character constitutes a person's highest good

   b: the theological doctrine that a state of freedom from sin is attainable on earth

2. a disposition to regard anything short of perfection as unacceptable

Unrealistic goals of perfection are unattainable and set us up for failure. A common misconception is that perfectionists think they are perfect. It's precisely the opposite. Perfectionists believe that perfection is attainable, rejecting anything less. Consequently, they reject themselves and others, perhaps even the whole world around them. When we strive for perfection, we are essentially rejecting what is imperfect, and imperfect is painstakingly what we become. Remember, what we behold, we become. In rejecting imperfection, we behold it. What we become are the antonyms of perfection: flawed, inferior, second-rate, broken, bad, defective, faulty, wrong, damaged, atrocious, blemished, and inadequate.

When others would give me compliments, I would downplay them. My children would tell someone how good their cooking was, and I would doubt my abilities and worth, concluding I would never be "as good as her." I assumed because other moms were cooking delicious meals that they were better than me, even though I would receive the same compliments.

I replayed this comparison game in my mind, but I never matched up. "Their house looks like *Better Homes & Gardens* magazine," my children would proclaim in appreciation of aesthetics. But what I heard was, *She's a better mom.* Better because she can decorate? I know, it sounds crazy when said out loud. Compliments of how pretty another mom was would bring me to the delusion that I was ugly. Because, in my mind, pretty was somehow perfect. And there was only one spot at the top. I couldn't accept the fact that these trivial things didn't really matter. I desired to be the best at everything because the disappointment that came with being mediocre was miserable.

I didn't consider these women to have real lives. Believing the lie, I dehumanized them and saw what I wanted to see. I thought they were the ideal and knew I wasn't. I didn't acknowledge they were probably more like me than they would want to admit. They had to cook, clean, and stretch themselves between full days of revolving hats . . . mom, wife, daughter, friend, coworker, life group leader, whatever it may be that filled their calendars.

My thoughts would wage war against my own body. I questioned my purpose and what I contributed. I drew a blank every time. I thought my family would be better off without me. I wasn't actively planning my way out of this world, but I saw horrible visions and had thoughts that I should just blow my brains out. I settled for an idea less extreme and would daydream of drifting off to sleep . . . and never waking up, if you know what I mean. I knew logically that these thoughts weren't true, but it didn't keep me from believing them. These are a few examples of the distortion that went on inside my brain as I continuously chose to come into agreement with lies.

I knew God was good—*so, so good*, but I doubted He was good enough to fix me. I viewed myself as a broken mess not even God could repair. I wouldn't dare share those dark places with others; it would be too vulnerable. I feared rejection and shame. I feared it was all true. I believed I was crazy, and if I opened my mouth, everyone would know.

So I kept the dark, disturbing thoughts to myself. I tried to pray the thoughts away—or maybe it was more like wishing them away. I didn't recognize them as lies. I thought it was my divine makeup, and I hated myself and God for creating me this way. I didn't know how to bring the lies into the light through confession or how to combat them with truth. Ashamed, I stuffed them further and further down, becoming a prisoner to them. The truth is the rejection that came from within was the worst of all. I teetered back and forth between truth and lies.

PUNISHMENT OR PROVIDENCE

It was like I was in a game of tug-of-war between God and the devil. I didn't understand at the time, but many years later, God gave me a fresh revelation.

He reminded me of a story found in 1 Kings. Two women, who had just birthed children, came to King Solomon. One child had died during the night, and they both claimed that the living child was theirs. Without knowing who the real mother was, King Solomon asked for a sword. Then he gave an order. *Cut the living child in two and give half to one and half to the other.* One mother said, *Please, my lord, give her the living baby! Don't kill him!* But the other said, *Neither I nor you shall have him. Cut him in two!* Then the king gave his ruling: *Give the living baby to the first woman. Do not kill him; she is his mother.* (1 Kings 3:16-28)

God graciously, with healing salve, gave me a supernatural God-vision to see He had to release me into the hands of the enemy to prevent me from being completely destroyed. He was preserving my life like He had with Job, complete with distinct parameters for the enemy of my heart. I was His, and He'd be back for me. He knew this wouldn't end me but would grow me even more. What the enemy meant to destroy, God meant for good.

*"Skin for skin!" Satan replied. "A man will give all he has for his own life.
But stretch out your hand and strike his flesh and bones, and he will
surely curse you to your face." The Lord said to Satan, "Very well, then,
he is in your hands; but you must spare his life."*
(Job 2:4-6)

I was in the torture chambers of the enemy's camp. Are you familiar with torture tactics? They are precise and methodical. With every
poison-soaked dart, the enemy was injecting venom into my veins
until it altered my blood flow, clouding my mind and slowing my
response time. Even hope from the Lord, in the enemy's hands, was
manipulated and used against me. I knew there was a God, so he
made adjustments accordingly, tweaking the plan. Satan convinced
me to believe in God, whispering, *But if He really cared about you, He
would have delivered you by now. Nobody's coming. Nobody cares. They
don't even know you're missing.* Thinking back on this conversation
makes my skin crawl.

Even though I believed this, I continued to beg God for deliverance. Sometimes, the enemy would go too far. But as he witnessed my
demeanor change when a spark of truth was lit inside of me, he knew
it was time to pull back—at least for that day. War heroes are trained
for battle and put through the harshest testing. A single blow won't
get them to release top secret information. Nor does fifty blows to the
head, causing victims to pass out. The enemy wants their captive to
be awake to experience every labored breath as they suffer the monotonous, repetitive, annoying torture.

*But the eyes of the Lord are on those who fear Him, on those whose
hope is in his unfailing love, to deliver them from death and keep them
alive in famine. We wait in hope for the Lord; He is our help and our shield.*
(Psalm 33:18-20)

Whole blocks of my life went unrecorded in my mind because of the mind-numbing medication the enemy handed me. These weren't physical pills but invisible poison. My eyes were bloodshot and red, squinted and demented, though I grew to like the numbing and would even welcome it at times. This torture went on for years until he handed me the razor blade, leaving me alone to inflict my own wounds as he moved on to the next victim.

If you've ever struggled with a mind consumed by depression, you may relate with the concept that physically you don't have much to show for your time but you are exhausted from the mental exertion you trudge through each day. You know you're not lazy, but you still label yourself that way and beat yourself up for not being able to do more. Have you ever planned to do a list of things? You start out hopeful but are unable to complete them? Did you get overwhelmed? Did you put it all back so your brain would stop the vicious cycle and your chest would quit hurting?

Honestly, most of what I believed was a fabrication concocted in the lonely world of my mind. It wasn't true at all. I would put words in people's mouths, like I knew everything they were thinking. I couldn't escape the pinball machine of negative thoughts firing at me. They were like fireworks on the Fourth of July, except for the part where the blasts would cease at the end of the night. These unrelenting accusations spewed like the hiss of a snake. I would catch myself creating conflict, dreaming up what someone would say and what I would say in response. Conjuring complete conversations in my head? It was literal insanity! I would feast on them for days at a time, ingesting one negative thought after another. All the while, in another realm, God was battling for my life.

I'd lived so much of my life unable to escape the dark, oppressive clouds that hovered. I wondered if God would ever rescue me.

Even though the darkness consumed me, I was still able to hear God whisper, *It's time to rise up.* He was there defending my sanity. Somehow, I came across the book *The Battlefield of the Mind* by Joyce Meyer. Many of the books I have received were at the exact moment I needed them. Soak in this life-giving quote from her book: "We are not walking in the Word if our thoughts are opposite of what it says. We are not walking in the Word if we are not thinking in the Word."

Sharing the darkness I was in is embarrassing. But if it can help one person by telling my story, it will be worth it. Honestly, it was hard for me to love myself. But God never gave up on me, no matter how many times He had to rescue my soul. He is still teaching me how to love and honor the little girl inside of me. So if you can relate to the darkness I was in, I'm here to tell you, God is always looking out for you.

Let me point you to your very own knight in shining armor, one who will always fight for you. The conqueror of the world sees you and rescues you from the enemy. He delivers you and provides a resting place for you.

They will make war against the Lamb, but the Lamb will overcome them because He is Lord of lords and King of kings—and with Him will be His called, chosen and faithful followers.
(Revelation 17:14)

I saw heaven standing open and there before me was a white horse, whose rider is called Faithful and True. With justice He judges and makes war.
(Revelation 19:11)

THE LIGHT COMES IN

There was so much more to learn from God's Word, but I am thankful for these peace-filled intervals when the sun would break through the dark clouds of depression and shine in all its glory. These are moments I was walking in truth and could bask in it, like the veil was removed and the oppression lifted. The feeling of peace and contentment was like lying in the grass on a beautiful day, surveying blue skies for white, puffy animal-shaped clouds. I could lay there forever, in the sea of green, filled with flowering clover. I thank God for these special breakthrough moments of peace and serenity that deliver hope to keep going.

Life is riddled with ups and downs. The climb is the place where we will spend most of our lives, not in the valley of lows or the mountaintop highs. I'm beginning to realize the climb is active and thrilling, overflowing with possibility. There's friction that sparks something if we are willing to be present to notice it. We have to resist the temptation to let distractions hinder our focus. It is important for us to learn the truth so we can detect the lies.

Do not conform to the patterns of this world, but be transformed by the renewing of your mind. Then you will be able to test and approve what God's will is—his good, pleasing and perfect will.
(Romans 12:2)

HERE'S A PERFECT PROMISE

Satan is cunning and slick, great at what he does. A specialist, even best in class. But guess what? Our God isn't in his class! He far exceeds anything the devil could think or imagine. The truth is, Satan will never be what our God is. God is our Redeemer! He is our Love Story. Our Fortress when we are weak, our Strong Tower. He will never give up on us. Many years ago, He conquered sin and death on the cross for you and me. He is our lifeline. I truly believe if it weren't for God, I would have faced so many more difficulties on top of my struggle with depression. I'm simply trying to wholeheartedly express that God is our only saving grace—even through personal struggles. You won't be perfect and neither will your life. *But, instead of seeking perfection, embrace your imperfections and let God's grace grow you.*

PERFECT SON

Christ's heart breaks when we try to impress God with our performance. *Perfection is in the reflection.* The good news is, when we become disciples of Christ, we get to trade in our sin for the perfect Son, Jesus Christ. He is the way, the truth and the life. (John 14:6) A disciple is defined as "a follower or student of a teacher, leader, or philosopher." When we become students of the Lord, we seek Him for the answers. When we look into the eyes of the Father, we get to see ourselves through His eyes and how He views us. Remember, we become what we behold. So when we look to God, His reflection is shown in us.

I prayed to the Lord, and He answered me. He freed me from all my fears. Those who look to Him for help will be radiant with joy; no shadow of shame will darken their faces.

(Psalm 34:5 NLT)

For we know in part and we prophesy in part, but **when perfection comes**, *the imperfect disappears. When I was a child, I talked like a child, I thought like a child, I reasoned like a child. When I became a man, I put childish ways behind me. Now we see but a poor reflection as in a mirror; then we shall see face to face. Now I know in part; then* **I shall know fully**,

even as I am fully known. And now these three remain: faith, hope, and love. But the greatest of these is love.
(1 Corinthians 13:9-13, emphasis mine)

The miraculous thing about God is there's enough of Him to go around. He is Omnipresent—always everywhere, Omniscient—all knowing, and Omnipotent—all powerful. He is patient with us as we grow and learn. And He is *for* us. If you ever feel alone and unseen, I challenge you to ask God to prove to you how He sees you. Ask for your eyes to be opened to the works of His mighty hand on your behalf. Read the following scriptures aloud and allow the truth of the Word to flood your heart.

I will extol the Lord at all times; His praise will always be on my lips. My soul will boast in the Lord; let the afflicted hear and rejoice. Glorify the Lord with me; let us exalt His name together. I sought the Lord, and He answered me; he delivered me from all my fears. Those who look to Him are radiant; their faces are never covered with shame. This poor man called, and the Lord heard him; He saved him out of all his troubles. The angel of the Lord encamps around those who fear Him, and delivers them. Taste and see that the Lord is good; blessed is the man who takes refuge in Him.
(Psalm 34:1-8)

Now that we know what we have—Jesus, this great High Priest with ready access to God—let's not let it slip through our fingers. We don't have a priest who is out of touch with our reality. He's been through weakness and testing, experienced it all—all but the sin. So let's walk right up to him and get what he is so ready to give. Receive mercy, accept the help.
(Hebrews 4:14-16 MSG)

Write about a time when you have given up on yourself.

Name friends, family members, or mentors who have encouraged you to keep going.

Have you ever considered that God was working through them on your behalf? How did that encouragement impact your life?

HEALING IS ON THE HORIZON. I have created space for you to journal what stands out to you through your story. Please don't skip this step, as I believe it is where we release things we didn't even know we were holding on to. Write something—anything. Healing is coming!

SONG INSPIRATION

"Love in Your Eyes" by Royal Company; "When I Lock Eyes with You / Your Love Is Extravagant" by Harvest

four

Not a Highlight Reel

*"Joy comes to us in ordinary moments. We risk missing out
when we get too busy chasing down the extraordinary."*

—Brené Brown

Have you ever hiked to the top of a mountain? Mountaintop moments are the reward for the difficulty you've walked through. The trek to the top is the challenging part. We should celebrate every blister and cut we acquire as we scale the mountainous terrain of life. But sometimes we only celebrate the mountaintop moment itself and don't give enough applause to the effort it took to get there. Atop the mountain, the views are expansive, refreshing, and thrilling—a place to rest and refuel. They're all picture-worthy moments to post to your socials. Each peak is designed to inspire vision and hope to sustain the continual journey ahead. However, mountaintop moments can never be experienced if we're not willing to make the climb.

Life is not a highlight reel, and really, thank God that it isn't. If that were true, we'd miss out on the many challenges we've overcome. Highlight reels are merely a compilation of success stories without showing the behind-the-scenes work of facing fears, stepping out of our comfort zones, and doing hard things. For example, have you ever considered traveling to another country? It can be kind of scary for some of us, but here's how I faced my fears.

A group from church was going to Haiti on a mission trip, and my cousin was prayerfully considering joining them. Shortly after, while borrowing my husband's Bible, a flier of a previous Haiti mission trip was stuck between the pages. In awe at God's perfect timing, I shared the news with my cousin, as it may have been a sign for her. A few days later as I went through a box of old movies to discard, I came across a DVD that went with the mission trip flier. Excited that this was another confirmation, I popped it into the player and waited to see what gift God had for her.

As I viewed the troubling scenes from this unfamiliar country and stories of redemption unfold, tears streamed down my face. A realization washed over me: the confirmations were mine too. God was leading me to go to Haiti, but my husband had conflicting opinions. Breaking the news to him went over about as well as a pregnant pole vaulter (as author Bob Goff would say). He emphatically said no. He even accused me of having lost my mind. I was disappointed and wondered if I misheard God. I was torn between the two and wanted to give due respect to both. At a crossroads, my earthly eyes couldn't see how it would be possible but trusted if it was really God's will, He'd make a way. So I waited patiently and prayed.

A few weeks later, the leader of the mission trip called, informing me it was the last day to reserve a spot. Hanging up the phone, I said a prayer I assume many newer Christians have similarly prayed in their walk with the Lord. *If the next song on the radio is "fill in the blank" (telling God what you want to hear), then I will take it as a sign to go.* It was a prayer of faith but absolutely misguided.

Needless to say, the song that I wished for didn't play. The call came while I sat in the parent pickup line at school, so the busyness of everyday life took over. Honestly, I completely forgot about the conversation and my prayer.

As our faith is built, we step out in bold childlike faith in prayer. God loves to see our desire in His direction even when it's done imperfectly. Sometimes, when we feel the Spirit's leading, we get confused, thinking God needs our help manipulating situations into existence. Remember, our God is not a genie God that acts on our demands. He does answer our prayers—just not always in the exact ways we might expect.

Later that evening while cooking dinner, my husband called for me to help him with something outside. While we were talking, he asked me, "Did you pay for your *thing*?" Sensing my confusion, he said, "Go ahead and put down the deposit to hold your spot." My heart leaped in my chest when the realization hit me that he was talking about the deposit for the mission trip! This may seem silly to some, but only God could have changed his mind. Also, how perfect of God to use the mouth of my husband to give the confirmation. When we are prayerfully patient, God never ceases to amaze us. Seemingly, against all odds, my husband willingly let me go to a country known for its poverty and corruption.

THE BEAUTY OF POVERTY

The weeklong experience in another country, surrounded by bodies of a different color, was one of the times I've never felt more alive. The environment was completely inconsistent with what I was conditioned to growing up. Most poverty in the United States can't begin to touch the deprivation levels in third-world countries. Advertisements on TV of how a penny a day can change a life can seem suspect and lead to the assumption that the pictured scenarios are either made up or especially isolated circumstances. But driving down the road, observing the expanse of extreme poverty, was an out-of-body experience. We couldn't wrap our heads around how our realities could be so vastly different when we are only separated by four short hours by plane. It was a tragic situation, yet in this case, somehow beautiful.

To witness people placing their trust in God in the midst of such despair was uncanny. The people we visited were caring and advocating for others when they themselves were in need of the simplest necessities for life, such as food and clean drinking water. A mattress to lay their head on at night was a luxury to even consider. They weren't only advocating to meet others' physical needs but also their spiritual needs. Haiti's most prevalent religion is voodoo, so the leaders were committed to carrying the torch for Christ, knowing that without God, these conditions would be fatal both physically and eternally.

It was humbling to witness such authentic faith and realize tangibly they had less than us, yet in other areas, they had so much more. One of our translators on the trip, a man named Seraphin, was a delightful person who quickly turned into a cherished friend. His heart was bigger than the world. Listening to him talk was inspiring. The vulnerability to his expansive dreams and clear vision for his community amidst his circumstances was a gift. We were shocked, humbled, and spurred by his audacious faith. He didn't only know the Word— he believed it so much that he lived it out every day.

Our eyes were opened up to deeper depths of relationship with the Lord. Our team returned home with such passion and desire for more of God. Changed forever, we couldn't unlearn what God grafted into us in those seven days. From one trip, opportunities to come alongside our new Haitian friends to make a difference were placed in front of us. We have been able to provide financially, build homes for widows, install water wells that quench thirst for whole communities, and purchase land for future projects, plus support individuals, families, churches, and schools along the way. We have been blessed to sponsor schooling and meals for multiple children living in under-developed countries monthly now for many years.

Hardships did come from the relationships that were built in Haiti though. Our eyes were opened to the extensive need and the inability to solve all their problems; it was heartbreaking. We tried to bring Seraphin from Haiti to the States so he could advocate for his people and find more financial support, but we continued to hit a brick wall. Do you know if you're from another country, getting a passport is next to impossible? Especially in a country like Haiti. It's not like in the US where you apply and receive one in the mail within a month or two. They petition, have letters written from people in the states, and still wait years to sometimes never receive one. The inability to visit their country because riots and governmental corruption was another serious challenge we had to face.

Making a decision between building on the relational bonds already created by visiting versus sending them the money it would cost to get there was a heavy burden. Each time the mail was opened to reveal a new sponsorship opportunity, it reminded us of worldwide depravity. We'd wrestle with the fact that we are unable to sponsor every good thing. Stress and sorrow comes with the understanding that as one family, we can only do so much. It's another reason why we have to continue to redirect our eyes to the Lord. He shows us the places we are called to invest in and carries the burden when we lay them at His feet.

RIGHT PLACE, RIGHT TIME

Another time God moved in our lives was when He organically positioned us for the opportunity to take a young, hardened sixteen-year-old boy named Katon into our family. We were not in the market for adopting or anything of the sort. Honestly, our plates were full with the schedules we already had with our two kids. But God brings beautiful opportunities to us when we least expect it, doesn't He? Katon and our son met through playing basketball together in school. We found out that he hadn't lived at home for over a year and had been sleeping at a friend's house in the meantime. Though they were able to provide a roof over his head, they were unable to fully take him in as their own. Vital roles were lacking, such as emotional support and an active presence at games and other activities in his life. We began bringing him to and from practices and games. The boys soon became inseparable. Literally, he started staying with us on school nights, which was against our rules at the time.

During basketball season, our schedules were crazy, so we were eating out almost every night. Since we had company, we indulged with sodas, appetizers, meals, and desserts. This was not the norm; it was usually water to drink and a shared appetizer or dessert for the family. We realized when he had been at our house for seventeen days in a row that we may need to consider what was naturally taking place. While considering the idea of taking him in, we took the responsibility seriously. He had not lived at home since he was fifteen and had already been through so much. Unwilling to injure him more, we knew if we were to go through with this, it would be set in stone and we couldn't go back on our word. He would be ours: the good, the bad, and the ugly.

Talking with a friend, I shared fears of mine that Katon might want to be with us because of what we could offer him materially. I had no desire to be someone's sugar daddy. I hoped he wanted to be with us because we were a safe place and our home offered him peace, not because of the indulgences he had experienced the last couple weeks. As any wise friend would do, she offered to pray over us.

The next morning on our way to church, instantaneously and without second thought, I asked Katon if he wanted to live with us. He said yes and that my husband already talked to him about it that morning. During the sermon, the pastor said, "God wants to be your sugar daddy." He then went on to explain how God wants to give us the desires of our hearts (Psalm 37:4) and God gives good gifts (Matthew 7:11). God caught my attention with the slang words from our pastor's mouth, and I left knowing how his message spoke to me personally. God confirmed our decision. From that moment, Katon was ours. God knew the desires of Katon's heart and wanted to lavish His love on him just as he does with each of us.

Katon had a different skin color from us, and people couldn't resist comparing me to Sandra Bullock in the movie *The Blind Side*. I can't say the accolades didn't tempt me to take credit, but none of this had anything to do with us and everything to do with God. Why did God choose us? Perhaps it's as simple as we were willing to say *yes*. Taking Katon in wasn't the easy choice. How do you let someone you don't even know move into your home, let alone become family? We had to take into consideration concerns for our daughter's safety, who was just a few years younger. Up until then, we had set great boundaries with our son's friends over the years to protect her from abuse—which is disturbingly more common than you think—and now we're letting a stranger move in with us.

We had to trust God in more ways than one. Some people thought we were crazy. Taking on the responsibility of an extra person, a misguided teenager at that, was strenuous and trying on all of our patience. More times than I'd like to admit, I was outraged by his disrespect to the point of losing my temper. Anger reduced me to a madwoman, screaming and throwing things. Adapting and learning to live with different cultures under one roof was eye-opening and diffi-cult. But without the difficulty, we wouldn't be able to tell you how embracing our cultures and learning from one another was humbling. Or that the opportunities to admit our wrongs and apologize were examples of love to him he'd yet to experience. It changed all of us for the better. It was a blessing we didn't know to ask for—we needed him, and he needed us. You can't imagine the amount of respect we see in each other's eyes now because of the trust we've worked hard for and built over the years.

NOT ALWAYS WHAT IT SEEMS

My husband has been a business owner for over twenty years now and runs a successful manufacturing company that supplies the needs of the cabinet industry. He's great at everything he does, from cycling to disc golf. He's a pilot, and we have our own aircraft. He loves our family unconditionally and would do anything for us. Without an inkling of a doubt, he's the hardest-working man I know and can accomplish absolutely anything he puts his mind to. You wouldn't know he has struggled with the fact that he doesn't have a college degree. Or that the thriving business we've built has taken his unrelenting dedication, rebounding through the literal floods and fire. Looking at him, you can't tell that he has torn both of his ACLs and is unable to compete in triathlons anymore. Or that over the twenty-three years of marriage, we'd fight and make up almost every day because at times he's been my archnemesis and at others he's my best friend!

It was amazing to witness our boys as leading scorers on the basketball team in high school—a dynamic duo, you might say. They won awards and were highlighted in the local paper after almost every game. They were strong boys with tender hearts behind their game faces. Both of our sons received partial scholarships for their achievements credited to their discipline and determination and went on to become college athletes. Looking from the outside, you wouldn't know the moments our son wondered if his efforts in sports would be worth it. If the hours of basketball practice he put in every day would even matter. And against what you might think, statistics show college students are some of the loneliest people and the distance away from home is sometimes scary for both them and their families.

Our daughter ranked in the top 11 percent of her graduating class and was chosen class president by her peers. She was part of the cheer team that made it to the top ten at nationals and was on homecoming court multiple years throughout high school. She and I got to experience a mission trip to Haiti together her sophomore year. She also received college scholarships for her academic achievements, not to mention that she is the most independent, mature, and wise teenager I know and is considered one of my best friends. But few people knew our daughter cried almost every day after high school, battling fear and anxiety just like I have. And that even though she was surrounded by friends, she still felt lonely at times. Still, she is an overcomer.

THE REAL STORY

The highlight reel is only part of the story. It's the portion of people's lives that gets celebrated by the world, but it's not the part in the middle where growth actually happens. The highlight reel is a product of making wise choices in the middle when the friction of life is difficult. Not the other way around. The point is the highlight reel is bogus. Sure, most of what you see on individuals' social media accounts are true facts not to be negated, but they are microscopic in comparison to the life that happens between. The value in the everyday grind cannot be appreciated in the highlight reel. Without pain, we can't treasure healing. The blood, sweat, and tears that once made you feel weak produces in you perseverance and discipline. You evolve, change, and grow in increments unseen, but when you look back, there's real measurable evidence. The middle, the uneventful monotonous grind, is where it's really at. It's the sweet spot if we will let it be!

YOU ARE THE ONLY YOU

If you are anything like me, I tend to compare others' highlight reels to my middle, which can cause a state of disappointment. When we laser focus on something, we are drawn to it like a moth to a flame. Too many times we get burned because we zone into the lies we so deeply believed. Comparison is a dream killer and a distraction from the mission. That's why it is so important that we renew our minds in Christ. (Romans 12:2) The truth is, you are the only *you* there is in this world, and God created you with purpose. Your life isn't supposed to look like anyone else's because you are his creation, unique in your individuality.

For example, a friend of mine who has no extravagant worldly titles can feel down sometimes when she chooses to focus on what's less important. But the truth of the matter is, she's a worshiper of God and a lover of people. She passionately walks in obedience to the Lord, sharing Jesus through talks on the phone and hugs in Walmart. She's gifted at speaking into the depths of people's souls. The Presence she carries is powerful. As the love of Christ exudes from her mouth, treasures are stored up in heaven. (Matthew 6:19-21)

GOD'S WAYS

If we can only remember that God's ways are backward from the world we live in. The first will be the last and the last will be first.

"For my thoughts are not your thoughts, neither are your ways my ways," declares the Lord. "As the heavens are higher than the earth, so are my ways higher than your ways and my thoughts than your thoughts. As the rain and snow come down from heaven, and do not return to it without watering the earth and make it bud and flourish, so that it yields seed for the sower and bread for the eater, so is my word that comes out of my mouth: it will not return to me empty, but will accomplish what I desire and achieve the purpose for which I sent it. You will go out in joy and be led forth in peace; the mountains and hills will burst into song before you, and all the trees of the field will clap their hands. Instead of the thorn bush will grow the juniper, and instead of briers the myrtle will grow. This will be for the Lord's renown, for an everlasting sign, that will endure forever."

(Isaiah 55:8-13)

That scripture is a beautifully poetic declaration from God. Because God's ways are higher than ours, He knows that when it rains, great things are being watered deep down to the roots of our souls. We, on the other hand, are susceptible to seeing the rain and believing it is only creating a big muddy mess we have to trudge through. There's a purpose to your pain even if you don't know it right now.

In what ways do you get discouraged in the mundane middle? Write as many as you can think of.

____

____

____

What do you think would change if you truly believed God created you for a purpose?

____

____

____

Take a minute to pray, asking God to remind you of your God-given dreams, and write them below.

____

____

____

What person can you share these dreams with for encouragement and accountability?

____

____

____

HEALING IS ON THE HORIZON. I have created space for you to journal what stands out to you through your story. Please don't skip this step, as I believe it is where we release things we didn't even know we were holding on to. Write something—anything. Healing is coming!

SONG INSPIRATION
"In Between" by Abby Siler; "I'm So Blessed" by CAIN

five

Vegas: It's Crowded Here

She gave this name to the Lord who spoke to her: "You are the God who sees me," for she said, "I have now seen the One who sees me."

(Genesis 16:13)

Upon arrival at the airport, I was hit with a profound sense of questioning as I scanned the crowd. Vegas offers a diverse assembly, full of charisma! But instead of feeling energized, I felt heavy. I'm sure you've experienced the hustle and bustle of any major airport, but Vegas is on another level. Slot machines in the airport invited people to stay awhile. Background noise from all the gaming permeated the room. Every one of my senses was heightened, tuned in, and almost at sensory overload.

There was a woman with a striking presence, wearing a sparkling diamond-encrusted bikini and pink heels, with a feather boa to top off the look. A man with a spray tan looked like he could be on *Magnum PI*. Homeless people sat outside the window, waiting for one of the lucky winners to spare some change. There was poverty and prosperity rubbing shoulders in the strange yet stimulating setting.

Coming off the heels of a mission trip, God had my attention. That experience set me up to have fresh eyes for the moment. I could clearly see through all the flashy masks. It was deeply disturbing to me because I knew what it felt like to run and search for anything to fill the void. You see, I had previously dealt with an "identity crisis." My compulsive need to make a name for myself caused me much internal damage. As I prayed in my spirit, God invited me to keep looking—not for the standouts but for the ones who get lost in the masses. He was highlighting ordinary, overlooked, and unpretentious people who otherwise would have blended in with the crowd. I suffered my own repercussions of feeling plain and simple. And since I was still on my own journey to find my true self, I knew God was using this experience to teach me another valuable heart lesson.

It was easy for me to see God loves and cares for the extreme ends of the spectrum, like those looking to the world to tell them who they are and those in poverty. But what about the everyday person? Those who simply blend in with the crowd? The disheveled young mom in worn-out leggings or that middle-aged woman wearing glasses? Is God concerned about them? What about you? What about me? Does God see us, and do we really *need* God?

ARE YOU HIDING IN THE CROWD?

Sometimes it's hard for me to comprehend God's sovereignty. How can He see those who desire to be seen and those who are afraid of truly being seen at all—at the same time? When there are no big problems going on in my life, I can assume God has more important things to be concerned with than my suburban issues.

Do you know what the best disguise is? Hiding in plain sight. I found myself in the company of those who fly under the radar. I was *comfortable.* We were able to meet our own needs and weren't in any visible need of rescue. My prayer life was minimal, and I was taking our easy life for granted.

Before going to Haiti, I was on the slippery slope of disconnection from God, heading for a complacent lifestyle. But I didn't see that until God opened my eyes. He took me outside of my little world and exposed my heart to His love. He spoke to me on the mission trip about the importance of staying connected to Him. Seeing the Vegas crowd of faces reminded me of my prior state of indifference.

Have you ever been in a crowd but felt alone? The feeling is worse than actually being alone. Hiding can come in many different forms. What about withholding your problems from a friend because they seem insignificant in the big scheme of all the world's problems? I'm not saying you have to share everything, but when we share with others, it gives them an opportunity to pray with us and help redirect our thoughts to gratitude. But be warned, the enemy wants us to feel shame and isolate ourselves from God and the wise counsel of other believers.

WHO TOUCHED ME?

The crowds flocked around Him like a hungry herd of cattle. I'm no longer referencing Vegas and its draw but the crowds that followed Jesus. Hordes of people crushed in around Jesus, following Him on His way to heal the dying twelve-year-old daughter of Jairus. Suddenly, the woman who had suffered with the issue of blood for twelve years pressed through the crowd. She believed in His healing power so much that she believed she only needed to touch the hem of His garment. When she did, she was immediately healed. Jesus asked, *"Who touched me?"* because He felt power go out from Him. (Luke 8:40-48) Verse 47 says: *Then the woman, seeing that she could not go unnoticed, came trembling and fell at His feet.* (Luke 8:47)

When she realized she couldn't go unnoticed by Jesus, she knew her experience went beyond healing. Jesus knew full well who had touched Him. He asked the question to give her an opportunity to come out of hiding. Healing is a powerful miracle, but it's the relationship with Jesus that is even more powerful. He leveled her up to fully engage in an up-close and very personal relationship with Him. And He was making a personal relationship priority over the healing He offered. He didn't single her out by her name but by her position. Jesus said, *"Daughter, your faith has healed you. Go in peace."* What healed her? She pressed into Jesus. Not only did she have a physical need but her faith drove her to press into Jesus for what she *really* needed. There is a blessing in the pressing.

Is He asking the same thing of you? Let's look at how important relationships are to Christ.

I KNOW YOUR NAME

Are you familiar with Zacchaeus, the chief tax collector? First off, let me point out that tax collectors were labeled as sinners by the Pharisees. Zacchaeus wanted to see Jesus, but since he was a short man, he couldn't get a good view over the crowd of people. So Zacchaeus climbed a sycamore fig tree (which represents clarity). And by climbing the tree, he was able to see Jesus.

From the crowd, Jesus looked up and gave His undivided attention to Zacchaeus. Jesus knew Zacchaeus by name, called out to him, and invited himself to dinner. *When Jesus reached the spot, He looked up and said to him, "Zacchaeus, come down immediately. I must stay at your house today." So he came down at once and welcomed Him gladly. All the people saw this and began to mutter, "He has gone to be the guest of a 'sinner.'"* (Luke 19:5-7)

Christ desires communion with us, and this scripture confirms that communion is not conditional on our status in the community or the opinion of others. *But Zacchaeus stood up and said to the Lord,*

"Look, Lord! Here and now I give half of my possessions to the poor, and if I have cheated anybody out of anything I will pay back four times the amount." Jesus said to him, "Today salvation has come to this house, because this man, too, is a son of Abraham. For the Son of Man came to seek and to save what was lost." (Luke 19:8-9)

It's important for us to get a clear view of Jesus, but the only way to clearly see Jesus is to know that we are *seen by Jesus*. What caused Zacchaeus to have a change of heart, to let go of everything he held on to so tightly? It wasn't the "righteous" people's judgment of him but a holy Christ, who not only loves but *is love*.

LET'S HAVE A PICNIC

In another instance, we find Jesus creating an opportunity to reveal Himself to many.

> *When Jesus looked up and saw a great crowd coming toward Him,*
> *He said to Phillip, "Where shall we buy bread for these people to eat?"*
> *He asked this only to test him, for He already had in mind what He*
> *was going to do.*
> (John 6:5-6)

It would have been impossible to feed the crowd without a miracle. But God can work with anything, even if it is five small barley loaves and two small fish (John 6:8-9). The innocent (and maybe even naive) child was simply doing what came natural to him—sharing his small lunch. But Jesus took the small offering and multiplied it to feed the whole crowd. Then Jesus said, *Have the people sit down.* When all the men had sat down, Jesus gave thanks and the disciples distributed the loaves and fish amongst them, as much as they wanted. *When we participate in a relationship with Jesus and willingly take a seat at His feet, we are satisfied and get to experience miracles we may have otherwise missed.* So be willing to sit with Jesus and listen to what He wants to say to you.

ARE YOU THIRSTY, GIVE ME YOUR CUP

Jesus sees the lonely and weary in the crowd and goes after them. For example, He knew the Samaritan woman would be at the well that day, knew what time she would be there, and knew she would be alone. He intentionally changed course so He could visit with her. This was unheard of because Jews did not associate with Samaritans. (John 4:7-9) Jesus is a rebel, rejecting religious laws because relationships are more important to Him than rules. And because of that, she experienced the living water of Christ and got a thirst-quenching drink that was better than a glass of cold water on a hot summer day.

Maybe you are weak, weary, or parched like the Samaritan woman. Jesus is never too busy to make a pit stop! He wants you to know that you are most precious to Him. We are all desperate for the living water He offers, whether we are aware of it or not.

Jesus answered, "Everyone who drinks this water will be thirsty again, but whoever drinks the water I give them will never thirst. Indeed, the water I give them will become in them a spring of water welling up to eternal life."

(John 4:13-14)

That spring of life welled up in the Samaritan woman, and she was so excited she couldn't help but go back to her community and tell everyone to *Come and see a man who told me everything I ever did!* (John 4:29) *Once again Jesus calls out the woman who had been hiding in her shame and uses her to share the gospel with others.* The Bible adds that Jesus stayed in Samaria two more days, long enough for *many more to hear His message and believe.*

Jesus made some personal connections in each of these miracles, and the crowds benefited by witnessing them or experiencing them for themselves. In these biblical references, we are taught that everything Jesus does is to bring us into relationship with Him. Has He ever set you up in the perfect position for an encounter with Him?

He sees us, knows us intimately, has compassion for us, desires to commune with us, satisfies our soul, heals and changes us—but only when we welcome Him into our heart. He creates opportunity, but we are responsible for taking hold of the miracle of a relationship with Him. When we do, we become His family.

The woman with the issue of blood went after Him, Zacchaeus looked for Him, the crowd sat down and listened to Him, and the Samaritan woman communed with Him. God is a God of relationship.

Have you hidden yourself in a crowd? Did you unintentionally want to disappear and go unnoticed? Many years before I had given Jesus my sin, I was assured of my eternal destination. But even though I've had an intimate relationship with the Lord for years, there are still times I feel disconnected and far from His presence. I don't know why I revert to hiding, but I want to learn to stay put and sit at His feet. And I want to help you do the same.

THERE'S NO NEED TO HIDE

No matter what has held you back or where you've hidden your heart today, simply come to Jesus. He knows and understands. You're seen, your prayers are heard, and He's ready to help you. There could be sin and shame in your life, but just come as you are. When you humbly step away from the crowd and have faith in Jesus, He will heal you.

Healing may take some time, but be willing to sit with Him and let Him love and hold you.

I've been a Christian for more than thirty years now, and my running from the Lord looks different these days. That doesn't make me a bad Christian; it just makes me a daughter in need. We are works in progress by God's grace. Whatever your need is, when you come to Jesus, He will mend your brokenness. When you do, it's your faith and belief in Him that heals you.

As I ponder the woman at the well, I always view this as her salvation—that she took a drink and was changed forever. But the scripture reference is in the plural sense. *Jesus answered, "Everyone who drinks this water will be thirsty again, but whoever **drinks** the water I give them will never thirst. Indeed, the water I give them will become in them a spring of water welling up to eternal life."* John 4:13-14 (emphasis mine) This verse encourages us to continuously drink from His living water and *remain* in Him. I don't know if I am alone in this, but God has to remind me way too often that I can do nothing without Him. I am grateful for that reminder!

Remain in me, as I also remain in you. No branch can bear fruit by itself; it must remain in the vine. Neither can you bear fruit unless you remain in me.

(John 15:4)

A BEAUTIFUL PARADOX

Have you ever watched an artist work on an upside-down work of art? During the process, the crowd tries to figure out what is being created without understanding the artist's perspective or inspiration. Just when they think they have an idea of what the picture might be, the painting is flipped over and, to the crowd's utter amazement, the intended design is revealed. Since it doesn't make sense that anyone would paint a picture upside down, we never consider viewing it from that angle. The gospel is the same way. It is a paradox, entirely backward from worldly wisdom. We think we understand, then God brings true revelation to us in aha moments—completely blowing our minds.

How can the God of the universe take time to care about a single individual? How can a holy God have anything to do with someone like me? The concept of Jesus is "stupendously fantastic," says one preacher. He is incomprehensible by the human mind. God, in all His power and majesty, humbled Himself to come into the world as an infant through a woman. Jesus came in this form to relate with us. He grew through adolescence and the teen years into a man without sin because He is not human but came in human form. He willingly gave His life on the cross so we could have life with Him through relationship with Him. There are so many examples of paradoxes in the Bible. We could cover people's insecurities, failures, and acts of pure evil, and we would assume to disqualify them from being used by the Lord. David was an adulterer and had a man murdered, yet God still considered him righteous. How can this be? David admits his sin in 2 Samuel 12, and he shows a repentant heart in Psalm 51.

We have a judge and an advocate, One and the same. I write this, dear children, to guide you out of sin. But if anyone does sin, we have a Priest-Friend in the presence of the Father: Jesus Christ, righteous Jesus. When he served as a sacrifice for our sins, he solved the sin problem for good—not only ours, but the whole world's.

(1 John 2:1-2 MSG)

The longer I am a Christian, the more I relate with the story of the prodigal son. At times, I am like the rebellious younger brother who wants the independence of an adult but not the responsibility. I want to live under God's protection but not His authority. I succumb to my flesh then run and hide. But it's not necessarily all about being *good*—like a performance—but it's about knowing where we stand as sons and daughters.

When I come to my senses, I return home, planning to confess my sin and unworthiness, just like the prodigal son. God, like the father in the story, comes *running after me*—even before I am close enough to be heard. He is filled with compassion, throws his arms around me, and kisses me.

Though I am not lost, I have an ongoing struggle with shame. I revisit this story as a reminder of His abounding love. However, there are also many times I am more like the older brother. He lives in the father's house with everything the father owns accessible to him and still questions his place. (Luke 15:11-31)

But as much as I relate to the sons in the story, I am also like the man on the pages of the book of Mark, who exclaimed, *"I do believe; help me overcome my unbelief!"* (Mark 9:24)

It's one level to know you belong to God, but it's another level of trust to live like a child of God. When I think about this from a human point of view, I think of my children. I hope they know they can come to me with anything. Even when I believe they are getting it all wrong, I don't strong-arm them and make them do it my way. I do my best to guide them in wisdom through love. God is even more gracious than we could ever be. He takes our hand and helps us stand back up, then He points us in the direction that leads us closer to Him. He is love, and love never fails. (1 John 4:16, 1 Corinthians 13:4-8) No matter how far you feel from God, He is painting a portrait of your life for His glory. Much like an artist who sees the finished artwork when he starts, God is creating a beautiful panoramic picture of His love and grace.

RELATIONSHIP TRUMPS RULES

In today's society, we hear a list of dos and don'ts that make up what many people consider to be the Christian life. What if I never allow alcohol to touch my lips or one perverse word out of my mouth? What if I become a saint, perfect in the eyes of my peers . . . then will I be righteous? The answer is no. When we look at the gospel through a lens of dos and don'ts, it's just that—a list of rules. But Christ came to completely set us free.

The gospel is extremely relationally focused. It is richly filled with an unmatched love for us to grasp. Once transformed by God's love, only then can we overflow. Love transforms every area of our lives, such as our behavior. If we miss this, we are just as blind as the Pharisees in the Bible. You might think the Old Testament Law and its impossible standards bring shame, but its intended purpose is to bring attention to our inability to do it on our own. Jesus laid the foundation of relationships with His unfailing love. He made it simple: love God and love others.

Paul wrote in Galatians 3:24 that the law was a guardian for God's people, pointing them to Christ.

Only Jesus can make us righteous. The gospel is less about our behavior and so much more about our relationship with the Savior. It is a miracle when we finally give up on working our fingers to the bone. We come to the conclusion that God was drawing us all along. Jesus came to reconcile us back to God and be in a personal relationship with Him. It's the perfect communion and restoration of a prodigal to the Father. It is finished. It is complete. It is perfect. What a relief that we have a friend and Savior in Jesus who really sees us.

Before this faith came, we were held prisoners by the law, locked up until faith should be revealed. So the law was put in charge to lead us to Christ that we might be justified by faith.

(Galatians 3:23-24)

God desires a relationship with you. Are you interested in going on a journey with Him?

____

____

What would you like to know about God?

____

____

____

____

If you are a Christian who has struggled with accepting the love and grace of Jesus, share how.

____

____

____

____

Write a verse that reminds you of the depths of His love.

____

____

____

Your Life Matters...

HEALING IS ON THE HORIZON. I have created space for you to journal what stands out to you through your story. Please don't skip this step, as I believe it is where we release things we didn't even know we were holding on to. Write something—anything. Healing is coming!

SONG INSPIRATION

"Palm of Your Hand" by Harvest; "Hold on to Me" by Lauren Daigle

six

Facing the Hater

*"Does your mind have control over you or are
you going to have control over your mind?"*
—Olympic Silver Medalist Galen Rupp

Maybe dreams are easier to ignore when they are kept inside your heart. Dreams are full of possibility but take action to accomplish. If our dreams don't come to fruition, negative thoughts can circle back to tell us a false story. Sometimes discouraging thoughts return without warning, bringing with them a spirit of heaviness. They catch us off guard, and there's not enough time to brace ourselves for the downward spiral of irrational emotions. "Why am I so broken?" and "Please *fix* me!" are once again our cries.

Are dreams for everyone? Does the woman cleaning the restroom stalls at the local mall make time to dream within her reality? Repeatedly, she is overlooked by people who don't give her the time of day . . . unless, of course, the stall needs cleaning. Like a recurring Groundhog Day, I imagine she goes home unfulfilled, only to wake up and do it all again tomorrow. No matter what our role is, we can coast through life at times, going through the motions until one day we look up and don't recognize our surroundings. Have you ever wondered what happened to your dreams? Or assumed your dreams were too far of a stretch for someone like you? We can shut down and stop dreaming without even realizing it. In our woundedness, we can harden our hearts to protect ourselves from pain. But when we do that, we also harden our hearts toward the Lord. If we are not careful, things from our past will come back to haunt us—things we thought we had overcome resurface again.

"No matter how much we know in any area, there are always new things to learn and things we have previously learned that we need to be refreshed in."
—Joyce Meyer

GOING THROUGH THE MOTIONS

Many things in life can get us off-kilter, stir confusion, or distract us. That's why it is so important for us to be in the Word and have true communion with the Lord on a daily basis, not just when we "need" Him for the 911s in life. The truth is, we desperately need Him every day, and it is prideful to believe otherwise. It's not our intention to go through life without seeking the Lord; it is simply habitual to walk through life in our own strength. It's our culture to trust in ourselves and countercultural to seek direction from God. For me, things can be going great with the Lord, and something as simple as moving to a new city can derail me.

Being the new girl in town, trying to connect with people who already have a core group of friends, can be difficult and isolating. Instead of looking to God for our worth, we look to others to tell us our value. Insecurities can rise at the failed attempts and contribute to feelings of insignificance or worthlessness. Surely, you've asked the questions, "What's wrong with me?" "Am I weird?" or "Will I ever belong?" In this kind of thinking, our minds are not on the things above. When we are looking at ourselves, we are not looking into the eyes of the Father.

Sometimes, even within a group of friends, a misunderstood word can lead to dissension, making you feel like the fifth wheel. Often, we strive in our relationships to be loved and accepted, never getting the results we hope for. It's possible the struggle we face is loving ourselves. When we are discontent in ourselves, we yield to the lie that others will always disappoint us or we will never be enough. Our eyes are once again focused on the wrong place.

DRIFTED FOCUS

Let's talk about comparison. We compare our marriages, homes, bodies, careers, and everything in between. Picturesque, Instagram-worthy posts have us circling. Judging from the "family" pictures, we put other men on pedestals, all the while tearing our own homes apart. Or glorify that desired body type we haven't had in years, reducing the opinions of ourselves to only what's skin deep. Or worse, we reduce the other person down so we can feel better about ourselves. We idolize the aesthetic home, or some of us just envy the tidy home that doesn't have dog slobber and Cheeto fingers on the glass door. I know for me, these examples of negativity or disappointment seeped into everyday life. I was so distracted I didn't recognize them as sin. I was a Christian, doing my best, taking the big, noticeable sins to the Lord but letting others like these slip through the cracks.

Considering careers or lack thereof, I wondered if other stay-at-home moms feared their school-aged kids will look back on them with disappointment. It's not a flashy life choice and can be lonely at times. When interacting with other adults, an innocent question such as, "What do you do for a living?" can make you feel small in comparison. If someone decided to ask, "What did you do today? You might say, "Oh, nothing much," believing what you had done was not important enough to mention. Insecure in our identity, we let the enemy discourage us and lose sight of our dreams.

Moving into midlife, big shifts of children graduating high school and leaving home can throw us into anxiousness. We fear everything we've invested our lives into is slipping through our hands. The little people we spent most of our time with won't be a part of our everyday lives anymore. Our children hold our focus for so long that parents often forget their own likes and dislikes. And as much as we want our children to spread their wings and fly, we fear being alone. How do we move on and function in this big world when our identities have been so wrapped up in parenting? We feel lost in our new roles with our young adult children. The silence that we wished for so many times when they were little now haunts us.

WHERE'S THE PEACE?

Maybe you can relate with being off-kilter or the lack of peace. Have you ever thought you'd be further along by now, expecting your life would look different? Comparing ourselves to people with college degrees and other accomplishments—that have catapulted them into successful careers we don't have—can be an insult to our ego.

Bitterness breeds on. We say, "I want to be a leader, so why am I cleaning the restrooms?" Or "I want to minister to people. What in the world does sealing envelopes have to do with ministry?" We ask things like, "I want to be a skilled tattoo artist, so why am I fetching lunch, taking out the trash, and mopping the floor of the shop? What does this have to do with the creative art of ink?"

This is where we lose many along the way to pride and impatience. I've definitely found myself hindered by these thoughts. We all want results, but sadly many of us get stuck in stagnancy because we aren't willing to put in the work of waiting. Or we've been trained to believe it's hopeless. The process can be frustrating and exhausting—it's much easier to quit.

That's why the Israelites, after deliverance from Egypt, wanted to return to slavery when things started to look bleak. They were trapped between Pharaoh's army and the Red Sea and saw no way out. They grumbled and complained and did not trust God. What they didn't know was God could have brought them a shorter way, but that route would have consisted of war . . . and He knew they weren't strong enough to handle combat just yet. (Exodus 13:17-18) In reality, they were complaining about God's providence because they didn't understand God's plan. He was training them to trust Him through each step of the journey.

Have you ever heard the saying "You can take the Israelites out of Egypt but it takes time to get Egypt out of the Israelites"? Experiences can affect our beliefs, and our beliefs affect everything else. The Israelites were controlled by a fear mindset because of their past experiences. (Exodus 14:1-12, 16:2-3)

In the psychological world, this is considered chained elephant syndrome or learned helplessness. The backstory goes like this: A young boy was at the circus. He was amazed by all the animals but especially the large elephants. He couldn't understand how such a strong and powerful animal was being held by a single rope around his leg that he could easily break. The boy asked the trainer why the elephant didn't break free. The trainer explained that when the elephant was small, the rope was strong enough to hold him so that when he would try to escape, he couldn't. The repeated failure to escape trained the elephant to quit trying, to lose hope, and believe he would never be free.

NOT HOW IT'S SUPPOSED TO BE

Here's one small example of what learned helplessness looked like in my life. Due to the circumstances of my upbringing, I wasn't the most confident or intelligent person growing up. When people would laugh at what I would say or interrupt me, it wounded me deeply. When I would share my opinions that others disagreed with, some would induce shame for not agreeing with them. From experiences like these, I learned that my voice didn't matter. It was the Southern saying, "Bless her heart." A buildup of little scenarios can discourage us and make us feel hopeless. More serious examples of verbal, physical, or mental abuse would only heighten feelings of desperation.

Do you feel like a chained elephant? If you are weak in your understanding, you can quickly lose hope and faith in God's goodness. You can doubt anything good will come to you and blame others, and even God, for your problems. Continuing to view life through the lies is a pessimistic sieve that everything filters through. Not recognizing comparison, envy, and pride for what they are can bend you toward complacency or even depression. Life was not meant to be lived like the story of the chained elephant.

God was calling the Israelites out of slavery and into freedom, and He is calling us out too. If we identify with the helpless elephant in any area of life, we may still be giving the enemy a foothold. The good news is we have what we need to live free because God has already paid the price.

OUR STRENGTH COMES FROM THE LORD

God doesn't ask us to change in our own strength because He knows we can't without Jesus. Some of these sinful thoughts are more recognizable than others. However, many of them slip through the cracks of our armor if we are not checking it daily. Without surrendering these negative thoughts to the Lord, they become bottled up within us and can cause physical stress on our bodies.

Our stomachs, backs, and heads hurt from the stress we carry, and we're depleted without understanding why. In hopeless seasons, we can have tendencies toward unhealthy lifestyles to numb the pain but contribute to even more health problems. We each have difficulties and can speak only of what we have experienced for ourselves, but no matter what our lives entail, there's common ground in that we each have to face the hater inside ourselves.

Have you heard the story of the two wolves? It's a great illustration of our struggle within. There was a man teaching his grandson about life. He said, "There's a fight going on inside of me between two wolves. One is evil, full of anger, envy, greed, self-pity, guilt, resentment, lies, false pride, and ego. The other is good, full of joy, peace, love, hope, humility, kindness, truth, compassion, and faith." He went on to say, "The same fight is going on in every person." The boy asked, "Which wolf will win?" The grandfather replied, "The one you feed."

The takeaway from this story is to ask yourself, *Which wolf am I feeding?* Instead of feeding into my dreams, I was feeding into my fears. While we are learning and growing, it is important to do self-evaluation and take inventory of what we are thinking, both positive and negative. Awareness is the first step to improving our lives.

PERSONAL INVENTORY

What do we see in the world that is a reflection of ourselves? Do we have a tendency to quickly assume things before knowing someone's intentions, or are we graciously giving people the benefit of the doubt? Are we kind or easily irritated? Do we see the good in people, or do we have a short fuse, complaining and grumbling, seeing only the negative? This scripture gets to the heart of the matter:

Test yourselves to make sure you are solid in the faith. Don't drift along taking everything for granted. Give yourselves regular checkups. You need first hand evidence, not mere hearsay, that Jesus Christ is in you. Test it out. If you fail the test, do something about it. I hope the test won't show that we have failed. But if it comes to that, we'd rather the test showed our failure than yours. We're rooting for the truth to win out in you. We couldn't possibly do otherwise. We don't just put up with our limitations; we celebrate them, and then go on to celebrate every strength, every triumph of the truth in you. We pray hard that it will all come together in your lives.
(2 Corinthians 13:5-9 MSG)

When I took inventory of my heart again, I wasn't excited about what God showed me. I was unaware how my negativity was affecting the world around me in devastating volumes. It was like the parable of the sower. A farmer sowed seed, but the seed fell on different soil—or different conditions of our hearts. Some seed fell and the birds ate it up. Others landed in rocky places not conducive to growth. Some were destroyed because they had no roots. Others fell among thorns that choked them out. Still other seeds fell on good soil. They came up, grew, and produced a crop, multiplying thirty, sixty, or even a hundred times. (Matthew 13:1-23, Mark 4:1-20) God was showing me that the seeds sown in my life were falling among weeds and getting choked out. Though the seeds sown had grown, they were weak and easily destroyed because they didn't have a healthy root system.

The seed cast in the weeds represents the ones who hear the kingdom news but are overwhelmed with worries about all the things they have to do and all the things they want to get. The stress strangles what they

heard, and nothing comes of it. But the seed planted in the good earth represents those who hear the Word, embrace it, and produce a harvest beyond their wildest dreams.
(Mark 4:18-20 MSG)

There was a holy sorrow, grieving for my ignorance. But God is a good Father, never leaving our side. The process of healing was painful, as with any form of recovery. God was still uprooting weeds of self-doubt that had grown for many years. Of course it was painful, but the reward of freedom has been so worth it. The point is that negativity is not the birthplace of dreams. To get our dreams back, we have to take our lives back. To take our lives back, we have to repeatedly hand them over to the Lord, who continues to restore us piece by piece. Sanctification is not a once-and-done circumstance but the practice of choosing again and again to put the Lord's will above our own. We can do this only when there is trust.

Once we've allowed the Lord to guide us to understand what's inside our heart, it is necessary to be honest and take ownership of the heart's condition. This is not to bring shame but to bring healing. Aware of the sin in our lives, we are then responsible for repentance.

My prophetic counselor, Rebecca Misek, has been an incredible resource to help me walk out God's calling, and I think you'll benefit from her advice too: "Everything carries opportunity. When you succeed, you have an opportunity to celebrate. When you fail, you have an opportunity to learn."

With the words we verbalize or the whispers we listen to in our mind, we are speaking either life or death into our situations. (Proverbs 18:21) Another scripture reads, *careless words stab like a sword. But wise words bring healing.* (Proverbs 12:18 ICB) Others mention *how good is a timely word!* (Proverbs 15:23) *The mouth of the righteous is a fountain of life, but the mouth of the wicked conceals violence.* (Proverbs 10:11) Read what Paul had to say to the Galatians:

> *Before you were led astray, you were so faithful. Who has deceived you so that you have turned from what is right? The One who enfolded you into his grace is not behind this false teaching that you've embraced. Don't you know that when you allow even a little lie into your heart, it can permeate your entire belief system?*
>
> (Galatians 5: 7-9 TPT)

The Bible says *wounds from a friend can be trusted, but an enemy multiplies kisses.* (Proverbs 27:6) Please be clear: negativity produces destruction.

I struggled with letting this little lie in for so long that it is now a mission from God to share with others that healing is possible. The enemy would love for you to stay in a negative mindset, unaware of its repercussions. The Bible also says, *The human spirit can endure sickness, but a crushed spirit who can bear?* (Proverbs 18:14)

If you are having trouble viewing these negative beliefs as sin, I challenge you not to take my word for it but humbly go to the Lord with your concerns.

> *All a person's ways seem pure to them, but motives are weighed by the Lord.*
>
> (Proverbs 16:2)

> *But the things that come out of a person's mouth come from the heart, and these defile them.*
>
> (Matthew 15:18)

A good man brings good things out of the good stored up in his heart,
and an evil man brings evil things out of the evil stored up in his heart.
For the mouth speaks what the heart is full of.
(Luke 6:45)

CULTIVATING DREAMS

I repented and asked God to take the reins in my restoration story. He restored my mind and gave me the ability to dream again. Dreams I had forgotten filled my heart, lifting my spirits and giving me a fresh outlook on life. God began restoring dreams, hopes, and visions for my friends in Haiti. I shared in an earlier chapter how meeting Seraphin on my first mission trip to Haiti affected my life. Our continued friendship has been one for the books. God restored my passion for helping the people of Haiti, and while I was only one person, God gave me hope and a vision to raise money on their behalf. I started an organization called Sustaining Haiti Project. I also stepped out of my comfort zone, sharing my experience of Haiti and their extreme need from the stage at my church. I prayed about a financial goal, and God gave me the number $10,000. The funds would purchase supplies to put up a fence around a property we purchased for the village and pay locals to do the work. That step brought us closer to fulfilling Seraphin's dream of building a much-needed hospital. The goal was a lofty one, especially since it was to a congregation of about a hundred people with half of that number consisting of children. But God is a God of multiplication! Miraculously, the goal was met by an anonymous donor.

Isn't that amazing? If I would have been unwilling to say yes to my discomfort and fear of getting on stage, a community would have suffered the consequences of my actions. We are still dreaming and hoping for the building of a hospital. We now have the land and the fence. We are waiting for God to provide what He desires next! Hope returned, and I believed my dreams were possible. In God's goodness, my joy was back, and I was having fun again.

FLIPPING MY DREAM

I had always quietly dreamed of flipping houses but couldn't see how to foster both responsibilities of being a stay-at-home mom and remodeling homes. Little by little, my dreams were cultivated, maybe not in the exact way I envisioned or on the specific timeline I thought, but I enjoyed dreaming again and was grateful. I began decorating for family and church events and found delight and growth in this area. Since then, I have designed the renovations on three of our homes and have helped friends with build-outs on space planning and design for their homes and businesses. Each experience has improved my craft. While flipping homes is not my career, God has grown my abilities and confidence in my talents.

At times I questioned if God cared about the design of our homes or if this was a worldly desire. But I know our environments affect our lives and was reminded that God himself is a designer. Not only did He design the whole world and our individual makeup (Isaiah 45:18 NLT), in Exodus He was the designer of the Tabernacle and gave others gifts of design and craftsmanship as well.

And He has filled him with the Spirit of God, with skill, with intelligence, with knowledge, and with all craftsmanship, to devise artistic designs, to work in gold and silver and bronze.
(Exodus 35:31-32)

I thrive on before and after pictures of restoration and light up at the simple thought of it. I get excited to discuss people's visions, and nothing compares to equipping them with the tools to make them happen. I've gone deeper over the years and have come to realize my passion for creating atmospheres, my gift to see potential, and the ability to pull it forward. God has paralleled the restoration of buildings and homes with the restoration of our souls and the atmosphere of our hearts, which I am even more passionate about. In doing so, He wove this book into my soul and inscribed the words on my heart.

Writing had never been a dream of mine, but God was preparing me for it along the way without my knowledge. It's beautiful and precious to look back and see His big-picture plan. He used the things I found great pleasure in, through journaling my prayers and conversations with God over the past fourteen years or so, to prepare me to write. I can see now how He was honing that craft as well. I believe God withholds some details of the dreams He's placed inside of us so we don't get overwhelmed, but we can keep in step with Him day by day and grow in His perfect timing.

THIS MEANS WAR

Let's not remain weak. We have a good fight to fight! In her book *Battlefield of the Mind*, Joyce Meyer wrote, "If you only do what is easy, you will always remain weak." Yes, we *will* trudge through challenging and heartbreaking experiences on the journey, but there's always beauty to be found when we redirect our thoughts according to the truth of God's Word and allow our faith to remind us that Jesus is our advocate. We must be patient, freely giving grace so we can grow even more. These are some of the steps I took on my personal journey to take my dreams back.

- Repented of my sins and righted my wrongs with the people God showed me. This was a humbling process for me but well worth it.

Therefore, if you are offering your gift at the altar and there remember
that your brother or sister has something against you, leave your gift
there in front of the altar. First go and be reconciled to them; then come
and offer your gift.
(Matthew 5:23-24)

- Made a pact with God. He would be the Teacher, and I would position myself as the student to learn. I surrendered my need for control and complete understanding. That's what faith is—trusting when we don't fully understand or have all the details. In doing this, we gain a teachable spirit and are equipped with wisdom from God.

Let me give you a visual example. When we allow God to be our teacher, it's like the movie *Karate Kid* all over again. Mr. Miyagi used unusual techniques to train Daniel LaRusso for the fight. He had him washing and waxing cars. "Wax on, wax off." Painting fences and houses. "Up, down." "Side, side." Daniel didn't understand why Mr. Miyagi had him doing these tasks. Come to think of it, I think he felt he was being made a fool of at one point. But if, like Daniel, we choose to trust our teacher, we will also reap the benefits.

Who, then, is the man that fears the Lord? He will instruct him in the way
chosen for him.
(Psalm 25:12)

- Added healthy outlets to decompress and release tension. Putting healthy options in place will help guard and protect us from defaulting to their unhealthy counterparts, such as drugs, alcohol, sex, gossip, zoning out with TV, or whatever it is for you. Our lives are not hopeless or beyond improvement. God will strengthen us so we are not vulnerable to sin. Creating healthy habits seems grueling in the beginning, but the benefits far outweigh the alternative. Author Mel Robbins gave this no-nonsense advice that has stuck with me: "That's what it takes to get what you want. Not big scary leaps once a year. It takes small, but irritating moves every single day." I have personally found physical exercise to be one of the most beneficial healthy outlets to release stress. It kick-starts our bodies with serotonin, which will help us in all other areas. Without energy, every task is more difficult.

The healthiest my mind has ever been was simultaneously the healthiest my body had ever been. When we work on our physical health, our mental health is getting a workout as well. God is in everything good, so let's not put Him in a box, assuming that He only cares about our spiritual growth. God wants us to be strong and capable in all areas of our lives. He created every facet of our being. Physical exertion will help us sleep better and wake up energized. Many times with exercise, chronic aches and pains are also known to improve, if not disappear altogether.

She sets about her work vigorously; her arms are strong for the tasks.

(Proverbs 31:17)

FLIPPING THE SCRIPT

There is a *why* behind every action, conscious or not. When our *why* changes, we are able to change as well. Training ourselves to practice positivity daily is necessary until it becomes a habit. Instead of associating negativity with our *why*, we have the ability to flip the script to a positive reason. Here's an example. Rather than approaching exercise from the negative mentality of "my body is weak," viewing it from a positive perspective might look like "my body will get stronger, one step at a time." Changing our *why* speaks into all viewpoints of life, not just exercise.

Here are other applications that have helped me along the way. Welcome the challenge to step outside your comfort zone and learn something new. Go to a counselor or apply self-development skills. Learn tricks like the five-second rule by Mel Robbins. When she was depressed and struggling to get out of bed, she came up with the idea to count down, five, four, three, two, one, and get out of bed. Doing this tricked her brain into obedience. The approach is elementary but simply life altering. I know because I also had to use this method myself. Small, intricate, seemingly minute changes can redirect the trajectory of our lives in such brilliant ways.

PRAISE BEFORE YOUR BREAKTHROUGH

Resist the temptation to shrink back and give up. Suit up for combat against the thoughts. Break the confining chains of oppression with the truth of the Word. And most important, have a grateful heart, no matter the circumstances. Psalm 28 is an example for us of gratefulness through distress. Just as the Lord saw David in his distress and had mercy on him, He sees us in ours and has mercy on us as well. Shout your battle cry through praise. Persevere through the process by remembering, speaking, and claiming truth for yourself. Believe every action step toward growth is bringing you closer to strength, growth, and wholeness. It's all worth it!

Praise be to the Lord, for he has heard my cry for mercy. The Lord is my strength and my shield; my heart trusts in him, and he helps me. My heart leaps for joy, and with my song I praise him.
(Psalms 28:6-7)

There's more to come: We continue to shout our praise even when we're hemmed in with troubles, because we know how troubles can develop passionate patience in us, and how that patience in turn forges the tempered steel of virtue, keeping us alert for whatever God will do next. In alert expectancy such as this, we're never left feeling shortchanged. Quite the contrary—we can't round up enough containers to hold everything God generously pours into our lives through the Holy Spirit!
(Romans 5:3-5 MSG)

Take a minute to pray, asking God what sins have slipped through your armor, and write down what He reveals to you.

____

____

____

Compared to the parable of the sower, what are the conditions of your soil (heart)?

____

____

____

If you are ready and willing, write out a prayer of repentance.

____

____

____

Ask God what healthy habits would be good for you to invest your time in to grow in other areas.

____

____

____

____

Your Life Matters...

HEALING IS ON THE HORIZON. I have created space for you to journal what stands out to you through your story. Please don't skip this step, as I believe it is where we release things we didn't even know we were holding on to. Write something—anything. Healing is coming!

SONG INSPIRATION

"Prophesy Your Promise" by Bryan and Katie Torwalt;
"RATTLE!" (feat. Tasha Cobbs Leonard) by Brandon Lake

seven

Embracing Broken

For you created my inmost being;

you knit me together in my mother's womb.

(Psalm 139:13)

had desperately tried to hide my brokenness and had gotten pretty good at it. Figuratively speaking, I had putty in hand, concealing my broken places with superficial patches, not realizing I was shutting myself into the confines of my own darkness. I labored, applying layer upon layer. Hiding became my full-time job. Because I wasn't okay with myself, I wouldn't let people see all sides of me. Pretending became the norm, and the overcompensation was cutting off my only air supply. I became a shell of the person I once was but knew that God had created me for more than pretending my way through life. Retreating was easier, and at the time, I thought it would be less painful. Trusting God is hard. I often wondered, "What if he doesn't show up?"

The Bible is riddled with broken people God used, and the overarching theme can be summed up in a simple truth.

Jesus replied, "'Love the Lord your God with all your heart and with all your soul and with all your mind.' This is the first and greatest commandment. And the second is like it: 'Love your neighbor as yourself.' All the Law and the Prophets hang on these two commandments."

(Matthew 22:37-40)

Why do we not grasp this concept? Why do we associate broken with bad? The truth is, we impact people's lives every day whether we want to or not. Your existence is important, and there is value in your life. Don't get caught up in all the fine details; remember to keep it simple and start with these two commandments in Matthew 22. Because if the enemy can capture your focus on the wrong things, his job is much easier. There will be inconsistencies along the way. We will fall, but God will never leave us. We need to be quick to repent and eager to receive His grace. The better we get at this for ourselves, the better we will be at giving grace to others as well.

Encourage yourself with this strategy

Each chop at the enemy you take weakens him.

Each blow says you don't accept the lies.

Each swing is your battle cry.

NEVER GIVE UP!

Who's ready to begin again?

It's gonna take blood, sweat, and tears. You will get a little dirty, but in the end, with God, you walk away carrying the head of your enemy! So you are broken. Good! That means there's more room for God's light to shine even brighter. Nothing gets wasted. He uses every broken piece down to the fine, splintery shards.

We look at ourselves and see brokenness. Yet God chooses to use broken vessels so His light can shine ever so brightly and we can be fulfilled in His wholeness.

But we have this treasure in jars of clay to show that this all-surpassing power is from God and not from us.

(2 Corinthians 4:7)

FAITHFUL TO HIS PROMISE

God was, is, and always will be faithful. Over time, through trusted friendships and safe places to land, God continued working to repair my heart. Unlike medical surgeons, God is not hindered by human limitations or restraints of time. He is patient and faithful and never quits. He sweetly continued to dissolve the scales from my eyes that kept me deceived and ignorant to the wealth of His goodness and truth. One day, a friend of mine shared that the testimony of my vulnerability led her to embrace her own brokenness. It was beautiful how my story—that I wanted to keep hidden—was able to influence her life in such a beneficial way.

This was a breakthrough moment for me to understand how God was using me, even though I didn't consider myself worthy. I began seeing the fruit God was bearing through me and understood in a greater way the impact my story had on others. And even though I'm still healing, I'm learning the only way to true healing is through continual surrender.

GOD'S VISUAL OF FREEDOM

Just imagine a vast field of green as far as the eye can see. The sight of mature oak trees steals your gaze. Their branches stretch wide, casting great shade for a cool place of retreat. The leaves beneath are rustling on the ground, making their own kind of music. Can you see me? I'm in the distance, my white dress blowing softly by the breeze, and vibrant-colored wildflowers dance in symphony around me. My body faces the wind, and it beckons me to fully release. With my eyes looking to the blue sky, I throw my arms as wide as they will go and lean back. My eyelids relax and close. A joyful smile spreads across my face until full-on laughter breaks out as I begin to twirl. Peace comes over me, and I rest in the tender touch from the Father and give in to the unparalleled feeling of freedom. The sun kisses me with warmth until my skin glows. The earthy smell of the grass and the gentle aroma of honeysuckle's sweetness nearby fill my nostrils as I breathe in. I could bask in His presence forever.

In this visual, I accepted the responsibility to walk alongside others on their journey to healing. I was willing to use the gifts God had given me to help others, even if it meant I had to bare my brokenness. I was finally willing to risk my vulnerability, pride, and my ego. I knew others had impacted my life through small gestures of acceptance, kindness, and a listening ear. I realized it was time I stopped believing the lie that I was unworthy. Through this vision and relationships, God drew me closer and closer, wooing me into His arms to His heart and the indispensable freedom He offers.

If you only look at us, you might well miss the brightness. We carry this precious Message around in the unadorned clay pots of our ordinary lives. That's to prevent anyone from confusing God's incomparable power with us. As it is, there's not much chance of that. You know for yourselves that we're not much to look at. We've been surrounded and battered by troubles, but we are not demoralized; we're not sure what to do, but we know that God knows what to do; we've been spiritually terrorized, but God hasn't left our side; we've been thrown down, but we have not broken. What

*they did to Jesus, they do to us - trial and torture, mockery and murder;
what Jesus did among them, he does in us - he lives! Our lives are at
constant risk for Jesus' sake, which makes Jesus' life all the more evident
to us. While we're going through the worst, you're getting in on the best!*
(2 Corinthians 4:7 MSG)

THE GOOD SOIL

At this point, the things I logically knew had seeped deep down into my soul, and I was being transformed. It was no longer just something I knew but was now part of who I was. The revelation of our identity in Christ is profound. As we continue to seek His face, we will grow closer and closer to the One who knows us best. In doing so, we become more fully aware of the soul. Choosing to embrace my brokenness also brought me to the place of accepting God's mercy, grace, and forgiveness. I had to decide if I truly believed what I said I believed, surrendering it all.

*Let us hold tightly without wavering to the hope we affirm, for God can
be trusted to keep His promise. Let us think of ways to motivate one
another to acts of love and good works.*
(Hebrews 10:23-24 NLT)

I absolutely believe in God's redeeming power. He really does make beauty from ashes. I have also learned how I should forgive myself since God forgave me. It's hard to accept forgiveness and mercy when there are wrongs committed. Naturally, it makes sense in my mind that wrongs deserve punishment, but I am so thankful for our sweet Father who sees things differently and graciously and reminds us of His love. He whispers truth in our ears, strengthening us to redirect our thoughts so they are in line with His.

Instead, be kind to each other, tenderhearted, forgiving one another, just as God through Christ has forgiven you.

(Ephesians 4:32 NLT)

YOU CHOOSE YOUR THOUGHTS

We can let our negative thoughts keep us prisoner, or we can take them captive instead. We can wear the grave clothes around town, or we can walk in freedom. Our thoughts are like a rudder on a ship. We may think they are insignificant, but they direct us where we go. Proverbs 4:23 (ICB) says, *Be very careful about what you think. Your thoughts run your life.*

It's your choice—what's it going to be? I hope you choose to take thoughts captive and walk in freedom! But how exactly do you go about doing this? The first step is taking responsibility for your thoughts and understanding the choices made everyday impact what your mind's condition will be.

Just like our bodies change with exercise and healthy eating habits, our physical brain is capable of changing through healthy thought patterns. The brain is a magnificently complex organ. God created us in such a way that we can establish new pathways for our thoughts to travel. This does take effort and work on our part. I'm not encouraging worldly positive affirmations, but what I am recommending is God-affirmations. Because they are the truth, God affirms what He knows is true about you. We should test our thoughts and belief systems against the truth of God's words.

And we destroy every proud thing that raises itself against the knowledge of God. We capture every thought and make it give up and obey Christ.

(2 Corinthians 10:5 ICB)

SHIFTING OUR THOUGHTS

Brothers, continue to think about the things that are good and worthy of praise. Think about the things that are true and honorable and right and pure and beautiful and respected.
(Philippians 4:8 ICB)

Remember in the last chapter when I was talking about growth—how you don't see it in the present but you can look back on it and recognize the evidence of growth? There are some constants in the rules of life, time being one of them. We understand that changes take time. It's natural to expect if we want a mature oak tree in our front yard that it will take many years to get to that point . . . thirty to forty years, to be exact. But aren't they a beautiful sight? So, know that time is an underlying rule that everything in life is built on. There are many important lessons I have learned over the years, but I would like to share five of my favorite ones with you.

1. Commitment

Commit to the Lord whatever you do, and your plans will succeed.
(Proverbs 16:3)

We must be devoted to the life we envision for ourselves. Results don't just fall into our laps because we want them. If you've ever struggled with unhealthy eating habits or being overweight, or you have battled addiction, you know this to be true because you've had first-hand experience. This may take some time to figure out if you are used to running on autopilot or putting out fires as they come, but I promise it will be worth it. Making a list of short-term and long-term goals will be beneficial for you, because when you are dedicated to the result, change naturally happens.

2. Learning

Instruct the wise and they will be wiser still; teach the righteous and they will add to their learning.

(Proverbs 9:9)

Never stop learning! There is always something new to take from your experiences throughout each day. Try reading books on certain topics that relate to the growth you are working to achieve. Another way to learn is to intentionally consider your history and your responses. If you are committed to doing this, you will draw understanding as to why you have done things the way you have. Equipping yourself to make corrections where they are needed prevents you from repeating your past.

3. Discipline

So I run with purpose in every step. I am not just shadow boxing. I discipline my body like an athlete, training it to do what it should. Otherwise, I fear that after preaching to others I myself might be disqualified.

(1 Corinthians 9:26-27 NLT)

Walking out what we have learned is not always an easy feat. So we have to use discipline to train ourselves for the work. The definition of discipline is an activity, exercise, or regimen that develops or improves a skill; training. We especially need to acknowledge the word *develop* in the definition. *Develop* means to bring out the capabilities or possibilities of; bring to a more advanced or effective state. I know this may seem elementary, but sometimes we need to ask ourselves if we are going through life, skipping vital steps that unknowingly hinder our desired success. The best way to practice something is to create a routine or ritual. The fact that we have to practice to be able to develop something leads me to the next lesson.

4. Consistency

So now, beloved ones, stand firm, stable, and enduring. Live your lives with an unshakable confidence. We know that we prosper and excel in every season by serving the Lord, because we are assured that our union with the Lord makes our labor productive with fruit that endures.

(1 Corinthians 15:58 TPT)

I am convinced that consistency is the game changer. Many of us are able to do challenging or monotonous things for a little while but then fizzle out. We can't give up and quit. We may take two steps forward and one step back, but if we are consistent in this, we are still gaining ground. We cannot be so disappointed by the ground lost that we lose focus on what has been gained. The lesson of consistency is what I am using to write this book. Since I continued to sit down and write, I now have a book to show as the fruit of my labor.

Leadership expert John Maxwell wrote, "Small disciplines repeated with consistency every day lead to great achievements gained slowly over time." It doesn't mean taking on some rigid schedule that causes more stress and grief in your life but simple acts that allow you to enjoy your life more fully. For example, I have never enjoyed doing the dishes. But honestly, how long does the task usually take? If I'm being generous, probably about fifteen to twenty minutes. And once I begin, I might wipe down the counters while I'm at it. I have let a twenty-minute chore steal my joy all day because the responsibility weighs on me until I do it. Left to my own devices, my tendency would be to leave dishes in the sink two days in a row, all the while dreading and avoiding them. Why? I'm not saying doing the dishes will be fun, but tackling them early and removing them from the equation allows valuable space in our mind for more important things.

Here are a few more uncomplicated ideas to incorporate into your day—they have greatly affected my outlook. Try waking up twenty minutes earlier. I love this because it creates an opportunity to do quick tasks and not lose any allotted time to have coffee, get dressed for work, or whatever it is that you normally do. One simple task I like doing first thing in the morning is waking up and making my bed because it is straightforward and doesn't take much thought or time. It is an accomplishment I can feel good about. It's also crazy how such a rudimentary task can pave the way for more positive experiences throughout the day.

The second easy suggestion is downloading the Bible app and taking ten minutes to do a morning devotional. This is a great resource because it can travel with you wherever you go, so when you're vacationing, it's available, or if you're running late, you can listen to it in your car. The Word is alive and active, and it will not return void. So I encourage you to add this to your life to lift your spirits and get each day off to a productive start.

Let perseverance finish its work so that you may be mature and complete, not lacking anything.

(James 1:4)

5. Forgiveness

For if you forgive other people when they sin against you, your heavenly
Father will also forgive you.
(Matthew 6:14)

Forgiveness is one that is a little tricky—it has been for me anyway. I have thought I had forgiven people in the past, but really I was ignoring the pain. I would try not to think about it because I couldn't make people ask for forgiveness. I was under the impression that to be able to forgive someone, they actually had to ask for forgiveness first. I have learned this is not true. There is a sense of release that has to come before being able to forgive. I had wanted people to pay for their wrongs. Until I was able to release them from the consequences for their sins, I stayed in bondage of bitterness. I was finally willing to forgive and have compassion on my assailants when I remembered Jesus's words when He was being crucified: *Forgive them, for they do not know what they are doing.* (Luke 23:34)

"To forgive is to set a prisoner free and discover
that the prisoner was you."
—Lewis B. Smedes

Individually, these five lessons are great tools to have and will add so much to your life. Practiced simultaneously, they create somewhat of a royal flush for you in the game of life.

Take a toddler, for instance. Over time, the natural progression is they grow as long as their core needs are met. Remember time is the underlying rule that all things build on. As parents we are committed to helping them grow, teaching them how to become all they can be. Discipline and correction are necessary boundaries we set to help train and guide them. Consistency serves as a reminder of boundaries and expectations, and we've already learned a good reminder is never wasted. Lastly, forgiveness allows us to reset and start fresh.

In the same way that we do not expect a child to grow healthy if their vital needs are not met, we will not grow healthy and whole without intentional commitment. We have to learn and advance, sharpening our knowledge and understanding. We have to be disciplined, as well, to feed and nurture our own growth for maturation, the desired outcome. We cannot merely make a single correction and expect change, but consistent adjustments over time make all the difference in the world. And accepting responsibility for our wrongs and offering forgiveness to ourselves and others is the healing salve that brings freedom. By combining all these attributes, we build character, produce fruit, and in the end, reap a harvest.

Let us not become weary in doing good, for at the proper time we will reap a harvest if we do not give up.
(Galatians 6:9)

STOP TRYING AND START TRAINING

I fully know the struggle is real, but the word God gave me this past year was *focus*, and that's what I have achieved with His help. And if by this comment you are gagging yourself with your finger, just know that I have been there too! But seriously, focusing on God is the key to true spiritual change. Applying these lessons has greatly improved the quality of my life, but if accomplished without the Lord, they would still be lacking. I have gained much-needed confidence in my capabilities as I have clung to the Lord. I have been sharpened in wisdom and knowledge and cherish the opportunity to share with others to inspire growth. I have vastly matured through the uncomfortable and sometimes difficult practices of discipline and consistency. I have not walked perfectly, but I am continuing forward and am bearing fruit. I have peace over my mind through forgiving and accepting forgiveness. I walk upright, and though I may stumble, I do not forget my Father who is leading me. Through the Holy Spirit I am strengthened to redirect my gaze more quickly these days and always remember God's goodness is for me.

> *Therefore, since we are surrounded by such a huge crowd of witnesses to the life of faith, let us strip off every weight that slows us down, especially the sin that so easily trips us up. And let us run with endurance the race God has set before us. We do this by keeping our eyes on Jesus, the champion who initiates and perfects our faith. Because of the joy awaiting him, he endured the cross, disregarding its shame. Now he is seated in the place of honor beside God's throne.*
>
> (Hebrews 12:1-2 NLT)

Can you believe your brokenness is not too big for God? Write down the parts of yourself you think are too big for God.

____

____

____

Have you experienced freedom in the Lord? Write down a memory.

____

____

____

Are you willing to surrender and let God use your brokenness to minister to others?

____

____

____

Write a prayer of surrender.

____

____

____

Your Life Matters...

HEALING IS ON THE HORIZON. I have created space for you to journal what stands out to you through your story. Please don't skip this step, as I believe it is where we release things we didn't even know we were holding on to. Write something—anything. Healing is coming!

SONG INSPIRATION

"Canvas and Clay" (Radio Version) by Pat Barrett; "Make My Heart Your Home" (feat. Alton Eugene) by Maverick City & Chandler Moore

eight

The Cage Is Open

You, my brothers, were called to be free. But do not use your freedom to indulge the sinful nature; rather, serve one another in love. The entire law is summed up in a single command: "Love your neighbor as yourself."

(Galatians 5:13-14)

It was Easter Sunday. Because of my spiritual growth and a more mature understanding of the Bible and the Holy Spirit, I was extremely grateful for the story of Jesus. I saw how my story was (and still is) intertwined with His mercy and grace. He is the beginning and the end. Everything created was done so by His hands. Death came knocking at the door for the consequences of sin. But Jesus paid the ultimate price, bearing our sin and shame. Through His sacrifice on the cross and His resurrection, He has extended redemption to all who believe in His name and confess him as Savior. The journey of knowing Christ as my Savior and walking through the sanctification process has evolved each year.

Many Easter Sundays were not like this for me. Growing up, we were told about Jesus but in the way we were told about the Easter bunny and the tooth fairy. My childlike mind understood Easter more as a cultural tradition than about the cross. I'm sure we were told about the cross, but the heavily influenced media marketing Easter eggs and chocolate bunnies predominantly overshadowed the true significance of Easter. What do bunnies, chicks, and plastic eggs filled with candy have to do with Jesus?

This is an example of how we have allowed culture and traditions to influence our beliefs, dimming the real reason for Easter's hope. I'm not suggesting canceling your family traditions; I am simply using this as an example to express how easily we can be steered away from truth if we do not intentionally prioritize our awareness.

Worldly views have distracted us from Jesus, but religion has as well. I know this from personal experience and in viewing the lives of those around me. Before knowing Jesus, we lived with wild abandon, making mistakes and not worrying what others thought. We lived for fun, doing whatever we wanted. Because we live in a fallen world, you and I still get it wrong. Even Jesus's disciples got it wrong at times.

When someone is introduced to Jesus, evil is there, waiting for the opportunity to deceive us. The enemy is cunning, and he will use what is seemingly good, such as religion, to accomplish his deception. From that, we can be misguided and morph into behaved, polished citizens whose laughter has dissipated and whose voices have been quieted. We can become pious perfection on the outside, but our hearts are far from God. Or we boldly take a stand for what is considered to be Christian values but are actually based on religion and not a personal relationship with God. We idolize the written law instead of the One who created all. We see in the Bible that religion kills and only God can save. Before Saul's conversion, he gave approval of Stephen's death by stoning him. (Acts 8:1) Jesus warns his followers of religious heresy many times throughout the Bible. Here are a few examples where He rebukes the religious leaders (Pharisees).

Woe to you, teachers of the law and Pharisees, you hypocrites! You travel over land and sea to win a single convert, and when he becomes one, you make him twice as much a son of hell as you are.
(Matthew 23:15)

No wonder some people don't want to be part of any "church." Hypocrisy isn't a true religion. We have taken the bait and allowed the enemy to influence our behavior. Instead of repentance and grace—work mentality, religion, and culture control us, and shame steals our influence. The vibrant life Jesus offers gets sucked out of us like a deflated balloon. In the colorful world God created, we settle for black and white when religion distorts the truth.

When introduced to Christianity, there's a tendency to start off with false beliefs. We wear our best clothes to church to make a good impression, hiding the behaviors we aren't proud of and guarding our conversations depending on the company. Since we are taught that these things are bad and as Christians we "need to be good," we conform. There's a false assumption that we need to clean up our act before coming to God. I'm certainly not condoning behavior that does not bring glory to God, but it is important for us to know that hiding doesn't glorify Him either. Honestly, we can't hide from God anyway.

He knows our hearts and can't be fooled. Hiding is nothing new; this is exactly what Adam and Eve did in the Garden of Eden after they ate of the forbidden fruit and were made aware of their nakedness. But before they ate the forbidden fruit, the Bible says, *The man and his wife were both naked, and they felt no shame.* (Genesis 2:25)

In their sin, they were tempted to be God instead of following the order of creation. In everything, the creator always knows the better purpose for creation. We were created for intimate communion with

God, but sin separated us from that communion. This is expressed when Adam and Eve sewed fig leaves together and made coverings for themselves because they were exposed and felt shame before the Lord. Like Adam and Eve, we think we know best but all our efforts at hiding are in vain. Just a few verses later, our providential Father prophesies Jesus in the flesh and His plan to redeem His creation.

And I will put enmity between you and the woman and between your offspring and hers; he will crush your head, and you will strike his heel.
(Genesis 3:15)

First off, enmity is the state or feeling of opposition or hostility. Here, it's referencing the relationship between humanity and Satan. We can all relate to opposition in our lives. Next is the prophecy of Jesus. The offspring of the woman God is speaking of is Jesus himself. It conveys Jesus will crush Satan—but it won't go without a price. Satan will wound Jesus, but Jesus will crush him.

Watch what happens next. God makes them garments out of animal skin to cover their nakedness. Why would God make a covering for them when they already made coverings for themselves? The covering of fig leaves Adam and Eve created for themselves did not have a blood offering but God's "covering" does. It is poetic imagery foreshadowing the sacrificial blood of the Lamb, Jesus Christ.

The Lord God made garments of skin for Adam and his wife and clothed them.
(Genesis 3:21)

This goes to prove the point that we do not have the ability ourselves to cover our shame. However, it doesn't prevent us from trying. God wants all of us; He wants to be our best friend, our confidant. God is beckoning us to bare our nakedness before Him and stop hiding behind whatever coverings we can come up with on our own. He already fully knows us and sees us—we are His creation, remember? He is waiting for our willingness to be transparent with Him. He does not shame us even in our nakedness; we are the ones shaming ourselves. In the garden, after Adam and Eve sinned, they saw their own nakedness and hid. It wasn't God shaming them. At the moment of salvation, the acceptance of God's providential covering through Christ, we are justified holy because Jesus is holy. God wants to restore our heart to His, through sanctification, which is joining with God in accordance with His will.

Let us fix our eyes on Jesus, the author and perfecter of our faith, who for the joy set before him endured the cross, scorning its shame, and sat down at the right hand of the throne of God.

(Hebrews 12:2)

Therefore, there is now no condemnation for those who are in Christ Jesus, because through Christ Jesus the law of the Spirit of life set me free from the law of sin and death. For what the law was powerless to do in that it was weakened by the sinful nature, God did by sending his own Son in the likeness of sinful man to be a sin offering. And so he condemned sin in the sinful man, in order that the righteous requirements of the law might be fully met in us, who do not live according to the sinful nature but according to the Spirit.

(Romans 8:1-4)

Jesus came as the final atonement for our sins. We are no longer tied to the rigorous actions of the former Law. Following religious rules will never earn us a spot in Heaven. Thanks to Jesus, we don't have to continually bring a spotless lamb to the altar.

It is only through Jesus we experience true freedom.

For if, by the trespass of the one man, death reigned through that one man, how much more will those who receive God's abundant provision of grace and of the gift of righteousness reign in life through the one man, Jesus Christ!

(Romans 5:17)

When I was young, I didn't understand how Jesus took upon himself the consequences for our sin, becoming my sacrifice. It is a great story in itself, but I'm so thankful the story doesn't end there.

When you were slaves to sin, you were free from the control of righteousness. What benefit did you reap at that time from the things you are now ashamed of? Those things result in death! But now that you have been set free from sin and have become slaves to God, the benefit you reap leads to holiness, and the result is eternal life. For the wages of sin is death, but the gift of God is eternal life in Christ Jesus our Lord.

(Romans 6:20-23)

WE ALL NEED RESCUE

There are many deserving people with heroic stories who have thrown themselves in front of buses for total strangers. There are many other religions that worship gods who were once great but were ultimately delivered into death's hands. Then there's the One True God. He sent his Son to overcome the consequences of our sin, who rose on the third day, conquering death. Name one that carries that title. He is the only God to be compared with none other. He's the winner, the MVP; He shot the winning basket. The game is over, no second guessing this one, no instant replay needed! The crowd cheers, the Redeemer lives!

If you don't know Jesus as your personal Savior, there is no time like the present. There is nothing we can do to earn salvation; it was freely given as a gift to all who believe.

But God demonstrates his own love for us in this: While we were still sinners, Christ died for us.
(Romans 5:8)

The Bible gives a description of what salvation is.

*That if you confess with your mouth, "Jesus is Lord," and believe in your heart that God raised him from the dead, you will be saved. For it is with your heart that you believe and are justified, and it is with your mouth that you confess and are saved. As the scripture says, "**Anyone who trusts in him will never be put to shame.**" For there is no difference between Jew and Gentile - the same Lord is Lord of all and richly blesses all who call on him, for, "Everyone who calls on the name of the Lord will be saved."*
(Romans 10: 9-13, emphasis mine)

If this rings true in your heart, God is calling you. He reveals spiritual truths to us, even without earthly knowledge. If you are willing, I would like to lead you in a prayer of salvation.

Prayer:
God, thank you for sending your Son Jesus to take my place. Thank you for forgiving my sins and, through the blood of Jesus, making me

holy. I confess Jesus is Lord, and my heart may not fully understand, but
through faith, believes Jesus died for my sins and God raised Him from
the dead. Thank you for saving me, thank you for loving me. Continue to
reveal your truth to me through your Holy Spirit. In Jesus's name, Amen.

Now go and celebrate with a trusted friend or mentor about your life-changing decision! And remember to get plugged into a local church for more support in your next steps as a follower of Christ.

If you believe this, know you are on the winning team, my friend! The enemy may win a quarter, but we win the game. It's already written out for us. We know the ending. We are free to celebrate, cheer, and laugh. The enemy does not have reign here, but he will take what we give him. None of it is his. Our mind, will, and our emotions are not his. We must yell it from the rooftops. If you are a child of God, He reigns in you, extending His power to you through His Holy Spirit. Our team wins. Satan's team loses. Since He does not have power over us, let's begin living our lives walking in the victory that has already been given to us.

The weapons we fight with are not the weapons of the world. On
the contrary, they have divine power to demolish strongholds. We
demolish arguments and every pretension that sets itself up against
the knowledge of God, and we take captive every thought to make it
obedient to Christ.
(2 Corinthians 10:4-5)

REDEMPTION

We were created by a loving Father with a redemption story intricately woven within us. It's who we are as people made in the image of God—we were made for communion with Him. His created purpose for all mankind is relationship with Himself. Through Jesus we are reconciled to the Father.

I'm realizing now, all those movies I loved growing up weren't by accident. Every single one of them has a redemptive story line. The hooker that finds love and is rescued by her knight in shining armor. The unpopular, unseen girl is finally seen, heard, and fought for. As the famous line goes, "Nobody puts Baby in a corner." A "clueless" and misguided teen realizes she got it all wrong and things aren't always what they seem. And a stereotypical "legally blonde" bombshell is able to exonerate a sorority sister accused of murder. Why do we gravitate to these stories? We love rooting for the underdog. Man, I am a sucker for a good redemptive story when characters overcome against all odds.

Obviously, the movie storylines mentioned are coming from a worldly view of redemption and don't do justice to the only True Redeemer. Everything that is not authentic is counterfeit. It goes to show us that our heart's desire is for redemption—we just have a tendency to look in all the wrong places. I know God is redeeming lives now. It's what He does. It's who He is.

Every good and perfect gift is from above, coming down from the Father of the heavenly lights, who does not change like shifting shadows.
(James 1:17)

I have read so many growth books. However, I do believe I have gathered information from them all, so none of my searching was in vain. The individual points each one emphasized has shown me the truth. The truth is coming together to create a bigger picture now. Like zooming out on our phone, we can see the surrounding places on the map, not just what's directly in front of us. It's a bird's-eye view, where our vision is not as limited, and the beauty from this view-point instills hope in us. Just the same with you—you will not have all the answers when you finish reading this book; more so it will be a stepping stone to the next life lessons on your journey of growing, healing, and becoming whole.

WRITTEN IN THE SKY

An entry from my journal (a letter to my husband):

This is my happy place, this is where I am reminded that I trust you. I trust you to keep me safe, I trust you to protect me. Flying in the plane with you restores peace to my soul. The skies are blue as far as I can see, I breathe. I let myself meditate and ponder God's goodness to us both. I know there's a redemptive story with us two. Why do I trust you in the air with my life but I don't fully trust you with my heart? You are the best pilot I know. I envy how, when you want something, you go and take it without a doubt in the world. Your excitement and passion disturb me. The way you don't care what other people say is mind boggling. You are not shaken, you are not moved, except possibly in a faster trajectory to where you had already decided you were going. You know who you are, your identity is unquestionable. You are sharpened and strengthened by those who question your plan. It helps you consider things you haven't yet. It's eyes in your blind spots, it makes you better. I know and understand it's why you do the same with me. To strengthen me and bring me to the point where I am fed up and tired of the mundane. You challenge me to not be afraid of risk and to know for certain what I stand for. You want me to be unshakable. Because then, maybe you would be a little sturdier too.

After writing this in my journal, one portion of it kept weighing on me. I asked myself, "Why do I trust you (my husband) in the air (controlling an airplane) with my life, but I don't fully trust you with my heart?" These words brought me deep sadness. God began softening my heart toward my husband, revealing resentment I had held onto for far too long, ushering me to forgive him for things I held against him for more than two decades. God not only wants to restore us to Him but to redeem all areas of our lives. He gently corrects and cleanses us from anything that is not of Him. We can waste our lives away, complaining about other people so we don't have to focus on all the changes we need to make. But the biggest motivator for people to change is for them to see the change in us. Forgiveness has to start with us—that is the only person we can do anything about.

Praise the Lord, O my soul; all my inmost being, praise his holy name. Praise the Lord, O my soul, and forget not all his benefits - who forgives all your sins and heals all your diseases, who redeems your life from the pit and crowns you with love and compassion, who satisfies your desires to do good things so that your youth is renewed like the eagle's.

(Psalm 103:1-5)

FREEDOM IN FORGIVENESS

The light melody of my cell phone alarm gently woke me from my sleep. It was 5:00 a.m., but I wasn't groggy (an unfamiliar yet peaceful feeling). Appreciating the morning, I breathed it in for a moment then headed to the kitchen to start our morning coffee.

Returning to our bedroom, I lifted the covers and slipped back into bed next to my husband. I pulled him close and enveloped his body with mine. The warmth of his skin permeated through the front of my body as I pulled him closer. I held him tight and adjusted my body until no air was between us. I rested in the quiet while he soundly slept, and I thanked God for the gift of marriage, relationship, love, and family.

Meditating with gratitude, I realized I had done this ritual or some variation of it many times before, but something was different this morning. *The difference was I was different* because of the forgiveness I offered, releasing him from the bitter place in my heart. I closed my eyes in peace and appreciated the simplicity of breathing in and out and feeling the results of his chest doing the same. I was at complete rest. For the next hour, I held my gift God gave me. I tried to comprehend that circumstances had not changed yet I felt completely different.

The emotional baggage I carried around for decades was undetectable. The yoke of disappointment and shame weren't weighing me down. This shift in perspective was unquestionably from God; I knew it was credited to Him, and I was grateful. My heart was full as I was reminded of His goodness. I wasn't afraid of the future or the past but was simply inhaling the present moment. I relished God's glory. I was taking hold of the ground gained in my marriage.

"The heart that gives thanks is a happy one, for we cannot feel thankful and unhappy at the same time."
—Douglas Wood

REDEMPTION IN MARRIAGE

God began my husband's and my redemptive story a long time ago, and our story of redemption will continue until we are restored to Heaven. Our love story could not be wrapped up in a two-hour romantic movie, and neither could yours. Think of all the stories you could tell. We have loved each other for over twenty-three years now. There's no questioning that. Many of those years were spent speaking different love languages. Communication has not been our strong suit, but we have gotten better at it through forgiveness, faithfulness, and never giving up on each other.

God used our strengths and weaknesses and has created something beautiful in us. I believe if my husband and I wouldn't have struggled, I could have easily put him on a pedestal—but that is a place reserved for God only. I could have been less aware of my need for God and possibly settled for contentment with human love and passion. That's not what God has for His bride, and He will use all things to bring us back to Him so we can be restored to our first love. And in doing so, He rehabilitates our love with others.

And we know that in all things God works for the good of those who love him, who have been called according to his purpose.
(Romans 8:28)

Marriage is a gift that can only fully be enjoyed through transparency, vulnerability, unity, and forgiveness. The difficult years we faced don't compare with the peace and joy we share with each other today. God taught me how to fight for my marriage's redemption story.

Remember: Love is not a fight, but we must fight for what matters to us.

Above all, love each other deeply, because love covers a multitude of sins.
(1 Peter 4:8)

Redemption is simple; it's a free gift. Jesus says, *Come to me, all who are weary and burdened, and I will give you rest. Take my yoke upon you and learn from me, for I am gentle and humble in heart, and you will find rest for your souls. For my yoke is easy and my burden is light.* (Matthew 11:28-30).

In your experience, what worldly counterfeits have not satisfied your desire for authenticity? How have they fallen short?

____

____

____

____

What religious views have kept you from the freedom Christ offers?

____

____

____

____

What is your redemption story?

____

____

____

____

Your Life Matters...

HEALING IS ON THE HORIZON. I have created space for you to journal what stands out to you through your story. Please don't skip this step, as I believe it is where we release things we didn't even know we were holding on to. Write something—anything. Healing is coming!

SONG INSPIRATION
"Man of Your Word" (feat. Chandler Moore) by Maverick City Music;
"Spirit Lead Me" (Live) by Influence Music & Michael Ketterer

nine

Blindsided

He heals the wounds of every shattered heart.

(Psalms 147:3 TPT)

Have you ever been blindsided? We don't see it coming because we don't expect it and it is not directly connected to our actions; it is simply out of our control. It's like a freight train hitting you at top speed. There you are in life going about your business—and out of nowhere, it hits you, leaving shattered fragments of who you are. The damage and shock can take months, years, and even decades to recover from—but somehow we survive. We don't die when it feels certain we will. Surprisingly, God has built us to be quite resilient. We've heard many stories of these kinds of events that alter people's lives every day. I'm sure you have some of your own as well—or you will—because we all do at some time or other.

We've heard devastating circumstances of twenty-plus year marriages crushed from adultery. How does it get to this point? Two people are married for more than half of their lives so intertwined . . . and now one has decided to disregard commitment. It can send an individual into shock. Forever ties are broken so carelessly—it could bring anyone to the point of questioning their identity. The life we thought we had a handle on thinks we are professional bull riders and sends us into the arena to get trampled.

BRACE FOR IMPACT

My husband and a close friend of ours were involved in a small aircraft crash landing. I arrived on the scene shortly after it happened, unaware of the accident. As I viewed the crash, heard the sirens, and saw lights flashing on the emergency crew vehicles, I began praying in the Spirit. I frantically called my husband and was grateful to hear his voice on the other end of the phone. They indeed were the ones involved in the crash, and our friend was unconscious. I could hear the concern for his life in my husband's voice; he suffered more severe bodily damage and had a long journey of recovery ahead of him.

Sudden accidents like this can send a family into survival mode, especially when the victim is the financial provider for the family. Even though only one family member was involved in the wreckage, the whole family is affected by its impact. The children still had to go to school while their dad was in the hospital and were bombarded with questions they didn't have answers to. The mom had to hold herself together for her family and deal with insurance companies, all while keeping some sort of routine for her children. She spent her days beside a hospital bed, grateful for her husband's life but questioned what their "new normal" would be.

She knew her husband was strong but wasn't sure how they would overcome this situation. In this case, I could only wonder what trauma the father must have been going through as well. A man who feels helpless is a very sad thing to witness, even when he is championing the circumstances. When pain and worry are bottled up, loneliness is often the result. In efforts to protect our loved ones' hearts, we can shut ourselves off from our relationships.

Addiction is another storm that can turn our lives and the lives of loved ones upside down. But addiction doesn't begin with addiction. There's an unconfronted, unresolved conflict within that relentlessly searches for anything to stop the pain. When our internal trauma intersects with a drug that offers release, it's difficult to overcome. The person struggling simply wants to be numb because life can be too hard at times, but its adverse effects send loved ones through hellacious warfare. Helpless family members would give their lives to turn things around, but it's out of their control.

The aftermath of a child's life taken too soon can send parents over the edge. What do you do without your baby? How can you continue to go on? Why would God allow this? I believe this is a lifelong recovery that can completely be healed only in heaven. Feeling alone and wanting to isolate, numbing every part of yourself feels like the only way to protect yourself from the unimaginable reality of agony.

Living in a fallen world, we are all vulnerable and unprotected from these sudden explosions. Disaster does not take into consideration your faith, financial situation, job status, skin color, or absolutely anything else for that matter.

CANCER SUCKS

I remember back to this specific day like it was yesterday, even though it was over eleven years ago. My dad sported his usual white V-neck T-shirt with his trusted 501 button-up jeans. He always wore a sort of trucker-style baseball cap and never left home without the original black Chapstick in his pocket, along with a roll of wintergreen Certs. Being a carpenter, he kept a pencil stuck behind his ear because you never know when you might need one. He had such a way about him, and everyone who knew him loved him. He was the life of the party, always laughing and cracking jokes, even in the doctor's office that day. My dad was a silly man, one who made me feel fully loved. His hugs were the best, and his "glass half full" perspective couldn't help but rub off on people around him.

That day in the cold sterile doctor's office, my dad's life changed forever when he was told that he had lung cancer. Alarms sounded in our bodies, signaling it was time to fight for his life. We tried not to panic, but the "C-word" has a way of striking fear in most everybody. We knew exactly who to call and were grateful to be so close to the world-renowned hospital, M. D. Anderson. Immediately, we began scheduling appointments and braced ourselves for the journey.

Though I wished it was under different circumstances, I was glad to have this time visiting with my dad and my stepmom on the drive to and from doctor visits. I was encouraged by the care he received. Over the following months, there were highs and lows, receiving hopeful results one visit, and then in the next visit there were the not-so-positive results.

One day while at home reading my Bible, the Holy Spirit began leading me to different verses. An overwhelming feeling came over me while writing in my journal; I felt led to pray for healing. My stomach turned in knots. I was afraid, but I believed God was asking me to lay hands on my daddy and pray for healing. I felt the Lord's presence with me.

I recall that moment distinctly when we prayed over him in the hospital room. He was hooked up to so many machines that were sounding different noises. Beeps, exhaust of pressurized air, and humming of blood pressure machines switching on made us a little uneasy. Excessive clouds were billowing out of the holes in his oxygen mask and had affected his vocal cords until his voice had become very raspy. Our family held hands in unity and began to pray that if you have the faith of a mustard seed, then ask and it will be done.

I continued in prayer for my father to be healed. As soon as our daddy heard "Amen," his quick-witted response was "You have some balls to pray that prayer." (My dad always had a way with words.) He chuckled with a tear running down his face. But I believed God could heal, and I believed He would. After less than a year of all the prayer, surgeries, chemo treatments, and diet changes, my daddy was sent home on hospice. I wasn't devastated because I was still holding out for a miracle. Was that response a way of coping or denial? I'm still unsure. But I had peace in the decision to trust in God.

Not long after this, my father took his last breath here on earth in his living room, surrounded by family. It is an incomparable moment to see your daddy breathe his last breath. Turmoil stirred inside as we experienced fear of the worst happening right before our eyes. The heaviness of despair and disbelief brought a stillness and quietness in the room. My older sister, being a nurse, tried to prepare us and our hearts when signs of his body shutting down began to appear, but we weren't able to believe it.

I was shaken to the core, and questions began whirling like a tornado in my mind. Why did God allow this to happen? What in the world was God doing? Was this some sort of sick joke? Why would God lead us to pray for healing if He wasn't going to heal him? The next few days were filled with so many different emotions: devastation, despair, anger, confusion, and exhaustion. Everything we had to do in preparation for a funeral was getting done from the mental state of a zombie. Not only had we suffered the biggest loss in our family, but we had to move straight into picking out a casket, flowers, and a plot, so we were unable to mourn peacefully. Somehow, in the midst of our turmoil, God was able to whisper truth to me that came out in a poem I wrote, even though my flesh resisted in defiance.

Daddy

My heart hurts

And I am sick inside

But I am happy for you, Daddy,

For you have arrived.

You've made it,

It's a joyous day!

I can't wait till we can all be with you

In Heaven to stay.

You are surrounded by God's presence far and wide.

We can only imagine how beautiful it is there inside.

You have seen your Maker's face,

And I know you are basking in His glory,

His love,

And His amazing grace.

I look forward to the day

When we have all ran our own race

To see you again—

Your beautiful blue eyes

And your lovely, happy face!

Until then, we can only be thankful, with no regrets,

That God blessed us here on earth with your presence!

I love you Daddy.

GRIEF IS HARD

The visitation and funeral were miserable to get through. If I heard another person say "I'm so sorry," I was going to scream. I know there are no words that provide comfort in the time of such loss, but I just wanted to be alone. And honestly, the religious saying of "Death is the ultimate healing" felt like a bunch of crock. It was like pouring salt on the raw flesh of my heart. In anger, doubt, and disgust, I questioned, "Is this just something Christians say when their prayers aren't answered?"

In the weeks and months to follow, I isolated myself and even questioned God's existence. Like clockwork, I woke up every morning with a heaviness in my soul. The feeling was like stacks of bricks weighing hard on my chest. Reality of my dad's passing hit me in the face again and again. I had to remind myself to breathe through the pain, to get up, and go through the motions even though my body felt no sensation other than immense heartache. I couldn't understand how people could go on in the world like nothing had happened when mine was crashing around me. I wished life would just give us a damn minute to grieve before we had to get back to it.

Close friends came to visit, brought food, prayed, and kept me alive in those moments I felt like I might die or wished I would. I wanted to escape the pain of the gaping wound death had delivered. One day while my friends were visiting, in my lack of understanding, I uncontrollably cried out, "Where is he?" Tears flowed and my anger toward God expressed how deeply I needed Him. I couldn't bear it anymore. Thoughts of my dad in the ground, the terrestrial creatures of the earth, the claustrophobia, horrific images haunted me as my imagination ran wild in the darkness of the unknown. The loss, these thoughts, this valley was killing me.

Knowing my father had proclaimed Jesus to be Lord of his life, my friends shared scripture with me that helped me get through. The thief on the cross beside Jesus (who had most likely committed his act only a few days prior), before he was crucified said, *Jesus, remember me when you come into your kingdom.* Jesus answered him, *I tell you the truth, today you will be with me in paradise.* (Luke 23:42-43)

I was comforted by Jesus's word *today*. I was able to understand that my dad was truly with the Lord the moment he passed. And that fear was wiped away. Scripture gave me peace like a river, and truth was water to my dry bones.

WAVES OF PEACE

Slowly, I was beginning to heal. Losing my daddy was the hardest thing I've ever had to walk through, and the only thing more difficult would have been losing him and not having my heavenly Father with me through the roughest time of my life.

Knowing God has its eternal benefits but also benefits of comfort and peace that pass all understanding here on earth. I was dependent on God for every breath and to simply exist each day, and He was faithfully holding my hand. The truth of redemption is monumental, but His providential love that placed precious people by my side to walk with me through my dark valley of grief was just what I needed. He lovingly reminded me, until I believed it, that as heirs of Christ, we are new creations no longer bound by the rules of law. Though our earthly bodies will experience death, our spiritual bodies will inherit eternity in heaven.

Where, O death is your victory? Where, O death is your sting?
(1 Cor. 15:55)

COPILOT

It is my belief we can do many things on our own until we simply cannot. That may even be all the way up until our own days are coming to an end. I believe we will not leave this earth without being given the opportunity to believe in the Savior. A life surviving through enemy fire alone is only resilient for so long. It is inevitable that mental and physical exertion will catch up with us. There will be a point when we are off our game and need relief. This is where God comes in. While God obviously is the best pilot for our lives, that's simply not how He designed things. He has given us a free will.

Life is like a Boeing 737 that's not intended to be flown alone. And the way I see it, God is our flight instructor. He prepares and teaches us how to operate the machine of a body He gave us and how to navigate the storms in our lives. Yes, some storms are unavoidable, but others absolutely are. Although God has equipped us with many abilities, doing life alone is not one of them.

We need a copilot, because in life we carry other passengers with us—whether we like it or not. God gives us the Holy Spirit to act as copilot. He comes alongside us and is on the lookout for possible hindrances. He watches the gauges and has an extra pair of eyes, sometimes taking the yoke when absolutely necessary—but otherwise lets us land the plane. And even when we do have to go through the storm with God, we somehow survive.

Sure, if conditions are mild, we can trust an autopilot. It's when the storm builds before our eyes that we need more hands-on assistance. God has given us great responsibility to pilot our own lives but wants us to approach life together in unison with Him. If the pilot ignores the copilot's warnings, things could spiral out of control. When we get to this place in life, the wise words *Two are better than one* (Ecclesiastes 4:9a), really resonate within our being. We experience a true need for close relationships, a helping hand, a shoulder to cry on, people to trust, and a God who can bear it all. God has equipped us to do life well. He laid down His life so we wouldn't have to suffer for the rest of ours. But He is patient, gracious, and loving, and He gives us free will to decide for ourselves if we will trust Him. I promise He is a trustworthy God.

Two people are better off than one, for they can help each other succeed. If one person falls, the other can reach out and help. But someone who falls alone is in real trouble. Likewise, two people lying close together can keep each other warm. But how can one be warm alone? A person standing alone can be attacked and defeated, but two can stand back-to-back and conquer. Three are even better, for a triple-braided cord is not easily broken.

(Ecclesiastes 4:9-12 NLT)

CLIMBING OUT OF THE VALLEY

Shortly after my dad passed, something seemingly insignificant began to catch my attention. Wildflowers began sprouting up, covering the fields and ditches in a sea of yellow. The happy color reminded me of my daddy. I drove down the road, remembering all the wonderful moments we shared with our dad and the blessing he was in our lives. God was lovingly pointing to the hope we have in Him and that He brings beauty from ashes. Those little yellow flowers were love letters from the Father, and the walls of my hardened heart began to crumble in surrender, giving Him permission as the Great Physician to search the depths of my soul.

Restoration is His specialty. The next scripture was directed to the Israelites, but God's character never changes. And in Galatians it says if we are in Christ, we are also heirs to the promise.

I will give you a new heart and put a new spirit in you; I will remove from you your heart of stone and give you a heart of flesh. And I will put my Spirit in you and move you to follow my decrees and be careful to keep my laws.

(Ezekiel 36:26-27)

*If you belong to Christ, then you are Abraham's seed, and heirs
according to the promise.*
(Galatians 3:29)

God is a loving Father, compassionate and patient. He is Jehovah Rapha, a healing Father, who can soften even the hardest of hearts. We may not ever fully understand our darkest valleys, but we must never forget that God is there with us holding our hand, guiding us through them. Even in our anger toward God, He is generous.

*For I am convinced that neither death nor life, neither angels nor
demons, neither the present nor the future, nor any powers, neither
height nor depth, nor anything else in all creation, will be able to separate
us from the love of God that is in Christ Jesus our Lord.*
(Romans 8:38-39)

What has happened in your life that blindsided you?

____

____

____

In your life, what has been your natural response to unwarranted trauma? Is it to withdraw, isolate, numb, lash out, busy yourself, or avoid things?

____

____

____

Have you ever been angry at God or felt like a direct blow was some sort of punishment?

____

____

____

Has God made Himself known to you through your pain? Explain.

____

____

____

Your Life Matters...

HEALING IS ON THE HORIZON. I have created space for you to journal what stands out to you through your story. Please don't skip this step, as I believe it is where we release things we didn't even know we were holding on to. Write something—anything. Healing is coming!

SONG INSPIRATION
"Rescue" by Lauren Daigle; "Give Me Faith" by Elevation Worship

Valleys

"Mountaintops are for views and inspiration,

but fruit is grown in the valleys."

—Billy Graham

Though valleys are painful, they are the place that brings us to the end of ourselves. It's in the valley that we realize we are in need of a Savior, not only for eternal salvation but to save us from a life of selfish gain. I have to continually surrender myself and my will back to God, because if left to my own devices, it's mediocre at best.

If you're anything like me, you hold onto your life with white knuckles. The intent of our heart drives us. We can be delusional and satisfied being "good people." Distracted by the busy world around us, we become a herd of cattle instead of heirs of the King. By clenching onto our own desires or letting the world influence us, we lose the only true life we've been given.

Very truly I tell you, unless a kernel of wheat falls to the ground and dies, it remains only a single seed. But if it dies, it produces many seeds. Anyone who loves their life will lose it, while anyone who hates their life in this world will keep it for eternal life.

(John 12:24-26)

Until we completely die to self, we will continue to find ourselves in valleys. I'm not suggesting that every valley is self-imposed. Because we live in a fallen world, many valley seasons, like in the last chapter, are brought about from grieving a loss or external elements beyond our control. However, they are also opportunities for growth. So if life's circumstances have brought you to a valley, it's likely a perfect time to do some soul searching. Be encouraged by this: the valley always produces something beautiful.

FAITHFUL IN THE VALLEY

David, who wrote Psalm 23, is a notable example for us to follow in our troublesome days. He was by no means a perfect guy, but God still considered him a man after His own heart. David, both as a shepherd boy and king, had many experiences with desperation throughout his life. Some were brought on by himself and others from outside sources, which is not uncommon from what we deal with today.

When he was young, he was undermined and considered irrelevant even by his own family. (1 Samuel 16:6-11, 17:28-29, 33) Anyone accustomed to insignificance? After being anointed king by Samuel, he endured around fifteen years of waiting before becoming king. Waiting is not easy for any of us, but the way we respond in the waiting is important. He faced a giant battle with Goliath (1 Samuel 17:40-58), and you and I will have battles of our own.

He was separated from his friend Jonathan and went into hiding for fear of his life because of King Saul's sins. (1 Samuel 19-23) Suffering unfairly from pain caused by others seems to be something we are not exempt from. Even though David was pursued by Saul and had the opportunity to take his life, he refrained, not taking responsibility for Saul's fate but letting the Lord avenge him. (1 Samuel 24:3-13, 26:1-25) Are our hearts in the correct position to not get revenge when the opportunity is right in front of us?

David grieved much because of his own sinfulness. In fear, he took his life into his own hands rather than trusting in the Lord's protection. (1 Samuel 27:1) He took refuge among God's enemies (1 Samuel 27:5-7) and distanced himself from God's chosen people. (1 Samuel 27:12) Have you ever surrounded yourself with the wrong crowds? Once David became king, he took Bathsheba for himself and premeditated her husband Uriah's death. (2 Samuel 11)

We can look at our sin and believe it is beyond forgiveness, but the Bible suggests otherwise. The point isn't about how good we can be but how good God is. In David's latter days, he faced consequences for his sins, one of which was to release his dream of building the Temple to his son Solomon. (1 Chronicles 28:3) We will also face consequences of reaping what we sow here on earth. But David's heart never gave up on God for his own failures; it produced knowledge that he desperately needed the Lord and was incapable of anything without Him.

DAVID KNEW VALLEYS WELL

In Psalm 23, David is strengthened by remembering the character of God and his personal testimony of God's faithfulness throughout his life. While covering Psalm 23, my pastor pointed out, "David didn't just write stuff. He wrote about what he was experiencing." David's penned words of worship show interconnection to his experience with the Lord in each stage of life. He makes ten points to equip and sustain us through the valley.

1. *The Lord is my shepherd* (Psalm 23:1a): David had considerable experience being a shepherd as a young boy and pulled from that time to illustrate who God had been to him. The sheep trusted David as their shepherd, and David trusted the Lord as his. In John 10:14, Jesus says, *I am the good shepherd,*

I know my sheep and my sheep know me. David recognized that God was his Good Shepherd.

2. ***I shall not want*** (Psalm23:1b): The job of the shepherd was to protect, care for, and provide for his flock. The shepherd was faithful to meet all the needs of his flock. David's words expressed his understanding of God's provision over his life.

3. ***He makes me lie down in green pastures*** (Psalm 23:2a): Sheep are easily worked up and can become erratic if their conditions seem unsafe. The shepherd's presence alone offered peace and lessened the friction among the flock. Another way the shepherd provides rest is by leading them to their food sources. Endless vibrant green pastures that come to mind when reading this verse was not David's reality. In David's time, the lush land was used for farming, and the sheep could graze only after it had been harvested. So the only land available to shepherds was rocky and hilly, and it received very little rainfall. The wind would blow seed into the crevices of the terrain, then moisture in the air would nourish the little sporadic sprigs of grass. The shepherd also kept the sheep clean and healthy, lowering the number of irritating pests. With the peace the shepherd provided, the sheep were able to lay down and rest.

4. ***He leads me beside still waters*** (Psalm 23:2b): Sheep cannot swim, so this statement is so much more than God providing a water source. If the Shepherd led them to a rushing river, they would be at risk of drowning. The shepherd knows his sheep and provides for them according to their specific needs, just as God does with us. Many of the water sources were cisterns below the ground. The shepherd would lead them to the water, but the sheep would have to follow the shepherd into the dark place.

5. ***He restores my soul, he guides me in the paths of righteousness for his name's sake*** (Psalm 23:3a): The Shepherd not only cares for the sheep's physical needs, but he also meets their emotional needs. Because sheep tend to go astray, they can become cast, meaning they get turned over on their backs and are unable to flip themselves over. If left unattended, the sheep will die there. Only the shepherd can gently restore their upright position, taking great care so the animal does not suffer. The shepherd would gently massage the sheep's legs to generate circulation. Once the sheep is upright, the shepherd would then pull the sheep close, comforting it until it can stand on its own again. God's rescue and restoration were familiar to David, and we can be comforted by it as well in our time of need.

May the God of peace, who through the blood of the eternal covenant brought back from the dead our Lord Jesus, that great Shepherd of the sheep, equip you with everything good for doing his will, and may he work in us what is pleasing to him, through Jesus Christ, to whom be glory forever and ever. Amen.
(Hebrews 13:20-21)

6. ***Even though I walk through the valley of the shadow of death, I will fear no evil, for you are with me*** (Psalm 23:4a): In David's declaration, he demonstrates remarkable faith in God's presence. This is not merely intellectual knowledge but a belief that has grown throughout his years in relationship with the Lord. Though valleys are not for the faint of heart and were not intended for prolonged stays, they are inevitable. But still, we have been called to walk out whatever is before us and not set up camp in the valley.

7. ***Your rod and your staff, they comfort me*** (Psalm 23:4b): Since many of us are unfamiliar with the role of a shepherd, we can assume that a rod and a staff are a form of punishment. But unlike herding, the shepherd simply leads from behind, keeping a watchful eye over his flock. He can see the ones on the boundary edges and gently reaches out his shepherd's hook to put them back on the safe path and keep them with the rest of the flock. Risking his own life, the shepherd would use the rod (a club-shaped weapon) to defend his sheep against predators. When not being used for defense, the shepherd would use it to gently nudge the sheep in the right direction. As the Good Shepherd, everything God does is for our good. He sees and knows what is best. The journey we are on might not seem easy or fun, but we can trust God has protected us from pitfalls. He goes to battle on our behalf, defending us against the enemy.

But David persisted. "I have been taking care of my father's sheep and goats," he said. "When a lion or a bear comes to steal a lamb from the flock, I go after it with a club and rescue the lamb from its mouth. If the animal turns on me, I catch it by the jaw and club it to death."

(1 Samuel 17:34-35 NLT)

(Note: The following verses of the Psalm seem to be in correlation with David's later years from experience as King.)

8. ***You prepare a table before me in the presence of my enemies*** (Psalm 23:5a): As king, David was very well acquainted with hosting dinners and entertaining his honored guests. Here, David was translating God's love and generosity. God had strengthened him to sit at the same table with his enemies—without fear—because God was with him.

9. ***You anoint my head with oil; my cup overflows*** (Psalm 23:5b): In Jewish tradition, it was customary for the host to anoint his guests on the head with oil infused with perfume as a form of utmost respect. Also customary was to give your guests a drink of water. Both the oil and the water were refreshing to the sometimes long-traveled guests. But here, David conveys that God goes above and beyond, not only providing a drink to quench our thirst but offering a continual flow that gives life.

You didn't take the time to anoint my head with fragrant oil, but she anointed my head and my feet with the finest perfume.
(Luke 7:46 TPT)

Jesus answered, "Everyone who drinks this water will be thirsty again, but whoever drinks the water I give them will never thirst. Indeed, the water I give them will become in them a spring of water welling up to eternal life."
(John 4:13-14)

10. ***Surely goodness and love will follow me all the days of my life, and I will dwell in the house of the Lord forever*** (Psalm 23:6): David recounted God's provision throughout his life and also prophesied as to what was to come.

Many people are familiar with Psalm 23 because, in our culture, it is read at both weddings and funerals. But have you ever given attention to Psalm 22? It is a mirror image of what Jesus went through on the cross. David writes, *My God, my God, why have you forsaken me* (Psalm 22:1), which are the exact words Jesus cried out (Matthew 27:46) while hanging on the cross. Verse 7 says, *All who see me mock me; they hurl insults, shaking their heads.* (Psalm 22:7) The same thing happened to Jesus. (Matthew 27:39) Verses 16 through 18 say, *they have pierced my hands and my feet, they divide my garments among them and cast lots for my clothing.* (Psalm 22:16, 18) When they had crucified Him, they divided up his clothes by casting lots. (Matthew 27:35) In verse 24, David says, *For he has not despised or disdained the suffering of the afflicted one; he has not hidden his face from him but has listened to his cry for help.* (Psalm 22:24)

JESUS HAS BEEN THERE

Similar to this is when Jesus was in the Garden of Gethsemane, He prayed, *My Father, if it is not possible for this cup to be taken away unless I drink it, may your will be done.* (Matthew 26:42) Jesus knew he was seen and his cry was heard by the Father. In obedience to the Father, He willingly took every valley we will ever face upon himself—every anguish, heartache, and sin. In doing so, the curtain of the temple was torn from top to bottom (Matthew 27:51), and all who believed in Jesus were able to go into God's presence for themselves. God doesn't remove us from the valley but does promise to be with us while we are there. If you believe in Jesus, you are not in this valley alone. The Holy Spirit is with you. And through Jesus's sacrifice, He provided for us an eternity without valleys on the other side.

Now it is God who makes both us and you stand firm in Christ. He anointed us, set his seal of ownership on us, and put his Spirit in our hearts as a deposit, guaranteeing what is to come.

(2 Corinthians 1:21-22)

TESTING OF OUR FAITH

Valleys can also be a time of testing. For example, when God tested Abraham with his son Isaac. Dissecting the biblical text, we see God says go to the region of Moriah. In the following sentence, He directs: *on one of the mountains I will tell you about.* The entire region was a very mountainous landscape, made up of mostly peaks and valleys. If we look back to Genesis 21, we see their journey began in Beersheba. This journey of testing consisted of a three-day trek from a low elevation in Beersheba along a valley between the mountains until they reached the mountain God showed him—which is unspecified, by the way.

Some time later God tested Abraham. He said to him, "Abraham!" "Here I am," he replied. Then God said, "Take your son, your only son, Isaac, whom you love and go to the region of Moriah. Sacrifice him there as a burnt offering on one of the mountains I will tell you about.

(Genesis 22:1-2)

Have you ever stood in a valley between two mountains? This reminds me of a time we visited a friend in Colorado, and she brought us to Seven Falls. Standing between the beautifully massive mountains, we were like tiny ants. To scale the mountain from this vantage point would have been almost—if not completely—impossible. The shortest route is not always the best one. When we stand in the valley between the mountains and give credit to God who created it all, we get to have an altogether different experience. Like Abraham, we can know the valley has paved the way for God's grace and has a purpose.

It is interesting that God would have Abraham and Isaac physically walk through the valley amid a somber time for Abraham's heart as well. Abraham's strength came from God, just as our ability to make it through the valley is directly connected to our dependence on the

Lord. Even in faith and obedience, Abraham was tempted to know the outcome. He wondered how God was going to accomplish this. The Bible says he questioned if he would actually have to sacrifice his son. Hebrews 11:19 says Abraham reasoned that God would raise the dead, so he must have thought he would have to go through with the sacrifice. But even though Abraham did not have all the answers, he trusted a God who did.

God doesn't test us in such ways until He has prepared us with the ability to pass the test. If you are being tested, it is likely God believes your faith will withstand the refinement. Not only will your faith withstand, but it will be strengthened in the midst of the test. God has a plan to bring us to new heights and build our faith. In His perfect timing, God provides revelation and purpose to each valley.

EXPERIENCE BRINGS GROWTH

Over time, Abraham's relationship with God proved to sharpen his faith through each valley experience. From the beginning, Abraham was considered righteous for believing the promise of God in his life, but even still, he got impatient. He and Sarah took things into their own hands, assuming God needed help with the promise. Abraham learned from his past with Hagaar and Ishmael that God does not need our help. God's promise still came through the miraculous birth of Isaac by his barren wife, Sarah, covering their many mistakes with His grace.

Abraham's faith was strengthened by God's faithfulness to the promise. It is the reason he was able to say to his servants, he and the boy would return. (Genesis 22:5) He believed God's promise that through Isaac, his offspring would be reckoned. He didn't know how God was going to show up, but he trusted He would nonetheless. And he knew God's way was always better. In effect of Abraham's unwavering faith, he was even able to say to his son Isaac, *God himself will provide the lamb for the burnt offering, my son.* (Genesis 22:8) And since he remained focused and steadfast, he received the blessing of God's dependability once again when God provided a ram in place of his son Isaac. Abraham called that place *The Lord Will Provide.* (Genesis 22:14) And to this day, it is said, *On the mountain of the Lord it will be provided.* (Genesis 22:14b)

Just like God did with Abraham, He takes us on a journey. Some of those journeys are long and some are short, but one thing remains true: He will test our faith and strengthen us even more through the climb. The evidence of God's faithfulness grows our faith to insurmountable heights as we travel to the mountaintop, one valley at a time.

Did you know that Jesus was also tested? The Bible says, after Jesus was baptized in the Jordan River by John, he was *sent* by the Holy Spirit to the desert to be *tempted* by the devil. (Matthew 3:16-4:1) In chapter 4, it says the devil took him to the holy city and had him stand on the highest temple. This is considered the Mount of Temptation. It goes on to say, *Again the devil took him to a very high mountain and showed him all the kingdoms of the world and their splendor.* (Matthew 4:8) Can you see the viewpoint of Jesus? He was looking at the holy city that was already His. *When he had finished praying, Jesus left with his disciples and crossed the Kidron Valley. On the other side there was an olive grove, and he and his disciples went into it.* (John 18:1)

Like David, I am familiar with premeditated sin. Have you ever planned to sin? Pray and ask God to show you if there are any unrepented sins. Write out your repentance below and allow God to begin healing those areas.

____

____

____

Name a time the Lord has been your vindicator.

____

____

____

If you are currently experiencing a valley, write out your unfiltered plea to God, and also the gratitude you have knowing God is with you and for you.

____

____

____

Has this chapter filled in any areas of questioning for you? How?

____

____

____

HEALING IS ON THE HORIZON. I have created space for you to journal what stands out to you through your story. Please don't skip this step, as I believe it is where we release things we didn't even know we were holding on to. Write something—anything. Healing is coming!

SONG INSPIRATION

"Hard Year" by Brandon Lake; "Graves into Gardens" by Brandon Lake

eleven

Wildflowers

"God writes the gospel not in the Bible alone,
but on trees and wildflowers and clouds and stars."

—Martin Luther

My attraction to wildflowers began the year I lost my dad. My love and appreciation for the blooms continued to grow over the years. Later, as I wrestled with self-identity, God spoke into my life again using wildflowers as a life parable. Though wildflowers are not usually in the running for flower of the year, they still stand tall for all to see their beauty sprinkled throughout the earth. They don't compare themselves to cultivated blooms like roses and orchids but shine in their individual identity, which is what God is trying to draw out of us. They're wild, vibrant, and unique, and we never see one standing alone. It's how we are in the body of Christ.

Have you ever compared yourself to others and honestly been disappointed in how God made you? The struggle is real. The imperfections, organicness, and hardiness of wild flowers lend themselves to strength. In God's goodness, He refreshes our perspective, matures our understanding, and reveals our resemblance to wildflowers—like an unfolding bloom of a brown-eyed Susan.

Consider how the lilies grow. They do not labor or spin. Yet I tell you, Not even Solomon in all his splendor was dressed like one of these. If that is how God clothes the grass of the field, which is here today, and tomorrow is thrown into the fire, how much more will he clothe you, O you of little faith!
(Luke 12:27-28)

Like wildflowers, we have many imperfections, and sometimes the conditions of our soil would certainly be detrimental to less hardy varieties of blooms. Yet the Gardener still grows and clothes us in His righteousness. Instead of staying stuck and disappointed that we aren't a rose, God gives us peace as we settle into the uniqueness He created in us. He graciously discloses his unconditional love for us and teaches us how to love and value ourselves.

We may fall short, but God doesn't compare us to one another. He simply asks if we're walking in true genuineness of who He created us to be. He calls our bluff on anything that doesn't align with His purposes for our lives. The only way we can accomplish true authenticity is by staying connected to Him.

Remain in me, and I will remain in you. No branch can bear fruit by itself; it must remain in the vine. Neither can you bear fruit unless you remain in me.
(John 15:4)

WEED OR WILDFLOWER

While searching the internet for information on wildflowers, some resources suggested wildflowers were weeds. Honestly, this information freaked me out! I asked God, "What are you trying to teach me God? Am I a weed?"

Of course, the enemy is always lurking, waiting for the opportunity to confuse and distract us from the truth. As I continued the search, other sources proposed that a weed is simply a plant that is considered out of place from a human perspective. For example, sunflowers are considered weeds by some.

This concept goes along with the history of the world. As humans, we take authentic things given to us by God in their beautiful natural form and try to perfect them, weakening their original makeup. While they may, in fact, be more appealing to the eye, they are genetically modified and weakened from their original purpose. God created us to be wild with abandon, but we are tempted by the world and by religion, in different ways, to conform to the perceived view of what is good and beautiful. *What if a "weed" could, in reality, be a wildflower in God's eyes?*

Another source reinforced the point God was showing me. While we admire flower blossoms for their bold colors, shapes, and scents, their main function is to make seeds for the vital process of reproduction. To this end, their blooms are designed to attract insects, birds, and even bats for pollination. Songbirds and butterflies especially seek out wildflowers. "They're a food source for these flying creatures, while cultivated flowers are not," says horticulturist and author Jim Wilson. It is of interest that, according to the *World Book Encyclopedia*, "originally, all flowers were wild flowers."

This makes me think of the gospel. If executed well, by surrendering to the Father daily, people would naturally be drawn to Christians for their life-giving qualities. Like wildflowers to songbirds and butterflies, we should produce a sweet aroma that attracts people to the love of Christ. Once drawn to us, we should be a place that provides nourishment so they can thrive. We cannot merely be something pretty to look at like a cultivated bloom, providing empty promises. Wildflowers may be weakened by wind and rain, but they are not destroyed because their roots grow as deep as ten feet.

May we let our roots grow deeper than surface level, gleaning from the true source that nourishes all, being made sturdy by the Gardener, exuding the sweet love of the Father, and bringing nourishment to others.

But thanks be to God, who always leads in triumphal procession in Christ and through us spreads everywhere the fragrance of the knowledge of him. For we are to God the aroma of Christ among those who are perishing. To the one, we are the smell of death; to the other, the fragrance of life. And who is equal to such a task?

(2 Corinthians 2:14-16)

BEAUTY UNFOLDING

Beautiful tattoos are intriguing to me. People's grit and confidence to mark their body forever is also shocking to me. With likes and dislikes changing daily, how does someone commit to ink in such a permanent way? But after the way God spoke through the parallel of wildflowers, my eyes were opened to the beauty He saw in me and His creation. I came to the conclusion that if I were to get a tattoo, it would be of wildflowers.

I am a rose of Sharon, a lily of the valleys. Like a lily among thorns is my darling among maidens. Like an apple tree among the trees of the forest is my lover among young men. I delight to sit in his shade, and his fruit is sweet to my taste. He has taken me to the banquet hall, and his banner over me is love.

(Song of Songs 2:1-4)

The scripture above is a poem depicting the love between a woman and King Solomon and goes on to describe how a marriage relationship is intended to be. In God's Word, Solomon describes the church (or body of Christ) as the bride and Jesus as the Bridegroom, so we can see how intimately we are loved by the Father.

The lovely picture God paints, brushstroke by brushstroke, imprints on the cerebral cortex of our minds . . . and our beings are forever changed. When we are finally able to forgive ourselves for not being perfect, we are released from those strongholds in our life. It is God who works miracles in us, and we get to relish in the work of His hands. It's a time of rejoicing in the Lord. In these moments, we can't help but celebrate His goodness with everyone around us. Yell it from the rooftops, maybe even get a tattoo . . .

There is some controversy on the topic of tattoos so certainly investigate for yourself. In my contemplation, I wanted to do right by God and please Him alone—not to act irrationally on a whim or act out of fear or judgment of others. Every intention was genuinely to be pleasing to God with my temple, so I began praying very specifically and searching the Bible for answers. Coming across scripture references against marking our bodies with tattoos, such as in Leviticus, we can hastily come to the conclusion that bodily markings are bad and sinful. However, if we read this in context, scrolling out a few sentences, we read the following.

Do not cut the hair at the sides of your head or clip off the edges of your beard. Do not cut your bodies for the dead or put tattoo marks on yourselves. I am the Lord.

(Leviticus 19:27-28)

This brings us to another question. If tattoos are a sin, is cutting our hair a sin as well? For more clarity, read the various laws in Leviticus chapter 19 for yourself. However, pay attention to this scripture in Hebrews.

If perfection could have been attained through the Levitical priesthood (for on the basis of it the law was given to the people), why was there still a need for another priest to come - one in the order of Melchizedek, not in the order of Aaron? For when there is a change in priesthood, there must also be a change in the law.
(Hebrews 7:11-12)

While all scripture is God breathed (2 Timothy 3:16), we still have to remember to look at the scriptures contextually. After studying for myself, I felt peace with the decision to get a tattoo. Please know this is not an advocacy for tattoos but my personal story. Each individual should take it up with God themselves, as I believe the answer to the question could be different for each of us. As it says in 1 Corinthians 10:23-24:

"Everything is permissible" but not everything is beneficial. "Everything is permissible" - but not everything is constructive. Nobody should seek his own good, but the good of others.

Peace for me, when prayerfully considering something, is a clue that God is not forbidding it. When we "prayerfully consider" (praying, asking for confirmation, patiently waiting for the next move), that prayer is honored and answered. Trust that God would make clear anything that is not pleasing to Him. As for me, many times clarity comes in the form of a settled or unsettled spirit.

Rejoice in the Lord always, I will say it again: Rejoice! Let your gentleness be evident to all. The Lord is near. Do not be anxious about anything,

*but in everything by prayer and petition, with thanksgiving, present
your requests to God. And the peace of God which transcends all
understanding, will guard your hearts and minds in Christ Jesus. Finally,
brothers, whatever is true, whatever is noble, whatever is right, whatever
is pure, whatever is lovely, whatever is admirable - if anything is excellent
or praiseworthy - think about such things.*
(Philippians 4:4-8)

*If any of you lacks wisdom, he should ask God, who gives generously to
all without finding fault, and it will be given to him.*
(James 1:5)

Walking in this peace, I reached out to many different artists for an appointment, and for some reason, each one fell through. So I interpreted this as another clue, a sign to hold off. It's important to listen for and trust the Holy Spirit's leading and follow accordingly.

*So I say, live by the Spirit, and you will not gratify the desires of the sinful
nature. For the sinful nature desires what is contrary to the Spirit, and
the Spirit what is contrary to the sinful nature. They are in conflict with
each other, so that you do not do what you want. But if you are led by the
Spirit, you are not under law.*
(Galatians 5:16-18)

Months later, a friend had a consultation with a tattoo artist and asked if I wanted to join her. Always along for the ride (considering this might be God's perfect timing), I was excited about the opportunity. After meeting with the tattoo artists, peace settled within my mind, and yet again, confidence about the decision arose.

I scheduled the appointment, continuing to pray until the day of to be sure I was not misunderstanding God. The fact of God lining up such a wild idea may seem silly, childish, unholy even to some, but I am thankful that God speaks to each of us in our own language. He is a very intimate and personal Father and gracious to answer our heart's desire to please Him.

Therefore, my dear friends, as you have always obeyed - not only in my presence, but now much more in my absence - continue to work out your salvation with fear and trembling, for it is God who works in you to will and to act according to his good purpose.
(Philippians 2:12-13)

The night before the appointment, God woke me from my sleep. He impressed on me to pray for the artist I had an appointment with the following day. Let's call him David. I couldn't quit praying for David for what felt like hours. I thought this tattoo was simply an outward celebration of my inner healing, but God was revealing everything He had orchestrated was for multiple purposes, so much bigger than meeting my need alone.

Now to him who is able to do immeasurably more than all we ask or imagine, according to his power that is at work within us, to him be the glory in the church and in Christ Jesus throughout all generations, for ever and ever! Amen.
(Ephesians 3: 20-21)

God told me not to get wrapped up in the design and micromanage the guy like I might have a tendency to do but instead ask him about himself. God was asking me to be vulnerable with a complete stranger.

When we step outside our comfort zone, people might think we are crazy. And the idea can be scary and nauseating. These feelings arise from fearing the opinion of others. I argued with God, "I don't know him. Why do you always ask me to do hard things?" But then confessed, "I will do it, as long as you give me the words."

THE BIG DAY

Getting ready for my appointment, I was nervous but expectant, remembering God is so good and faithful. I was willing to be obedient as long as He was with me. As I walked through the door, my body felt the influx of nerves. I shared the wake-up call with a couple of friends who came with me to the appointment, and I could feel their support.

David welcomed us and asked how we were doing. Through my fear, I blurted out, "I'm good, but how are you?" Then I awkwardly began explaining how God woke me up to pray for him last night. I might have even cried. Ugh, vulnerability is hard. But that imperfect act of obedience opened up a door for us to talk about God for the next four hours while he worked on my tattoo. It was a living, breathing story of God's unfolding providence. It reminded me God goes to the greatest lengths to show His love to His people. We're all given the commission to share God's love with those around us, but sometimes it is divinely positioned.

It just so happened, no surprise to God, that David was going through a valley season of his own. He shared with me some of his current struggles and a dream he had where he was stuck in mud. Through the influence of the Holy Spirit, a scripture came to mind to share with him. It was ad-libbed at the time, but I found it in Psalm 40:2 and read it to him as well.

I waited and waited and waited for God. At last he looked; finally he listened. He lifted me out of the ditch, pulled me from deep mud. He stood me up on a solid rock to make sure I wouldn't slip.

(Psalms 40:1-2 MSG)

THE HARVEST IS PLENTIFUL

I shared with David the background story behind my tattoo—how God brought me through my valley season. When I saw ugly, unimportant, and weak, God showed me I was beautiful, valuable, and strong in His eyes. Through our conversation, I found out David's family didn't have Bibles of their own. That's when the Holy Spirit impressed upon me to buy them their first Bibles.

Another fear arose, and I questioned, "This is too much, God. This seems a little excessive for someone I don't even know." But God persisted, so I gave in. I prayed about what Bibles to buy, which toy I should give to their son, all the way down to which wrapping paper to choose. Everything was intentional.

Some may consider this a mere coincidence, but I don't believe in the worldly definition of coincidence but rather what God says about it. Do you know that according to gotquestions.org, the word *coincidence* is only mentioned once in the New Testament? Other translations use the words *happened* and *by chance*. Here, it states:

"The word *coincidence* is used only once in the New Testament, and it was by Jesus Himself in the parable of the Good Samaritan. In Luke 10:31, Jesus said, 'And by a coincidence a certain priest was going down in that way, and having seen him, he passed over on the opposite side.' The word *coincidence* is translated from the Greek word *synkyrian,* which is a combination of two words: *sun* and *kurios. Sun* means 'together with,' and *kurious* means 'supreme in authority.' So a biblical definition of *coincidence* would be 'what occurs together by God's providential arrangement of circumstances.' *By chance a priest came along. But when he saw the man lying there, he crossed to the other side of the road and passed him by."* (Luke 10:31 NLT)

In the parable of the Good Samaritan, three people were divinely positioned and given the opportunity to be the *"good* Samaritan," but only one listened to the call. May our hearts be tender and obedient when the opportunity to share the love of Christ "happens" to arise.

For whatever reason, in that moment, God was specifically seeking out David to hear about His love and acceptance of him. God will continue to pursue David, just as He does each of us. In my life, I have sown many seeds to the flesh; however, I cannot accept the fact that getting my tattoo was one of them. For me, it serves as a reminder of God's infinite and unfailing love. And even in those times when I do get it wrong, God is bigger than my worst mistakes and has the power to turn it all around.

Since my assignment from God, David and his family have visited a local church, and we have stayed connected through social media and checked on each other throughout the years. Who knows how that gift may have impacted his life. We will not always get to see the fruit of the seeds we have sown, but we must trust that when God calls us to something, He will accomplish the rest.

I have been asked many times about my tattoo, and each time has been another opportunity for me to share the love of the Father that it represents—now in more ways than one. It was a beautiful experience! And while at the time sharing the gospel didn't come easy, today I am grateful to be God's fellow worker. God uses our valleys to help us have compassion on others. And He sends us out with that compassion to be His hands and feet here on earth.

And how can they preach unless they are sent? As it is written, "How beautiful are the feet of those who bring the good news!"
(Romans 10:15)

We are coworkers with God and you are God's cultivated garden, the house he is building.
(1 Corinthians 3:9 TPT)

Write down any revelations from God you have misunderstood about yourself and your relationship with Him.

____

____

____

____

How has this truth been salve to your wounds?

____

____

____

____

Explain what restoration feels like for you.

Share a time when God used your valley to help another in their time of need.

Your Life Matters...

HEALING IS ON THE HORIZON. I have created space for you to journal what stands out to you through your story. Please don't skip this step, as I believe it is where we release things we didn't even know we were holding on to. Write something—anything. Healing is coming!

SONG INSPIRATION

"Wildflowers" by Brandon Lake;
"God's Wildflower" essay by Bill Gaultiere

twelve

Bet on Her

That's why my cup is running over. This is the assigned moment for him to move into the center, while I slip off to the sidelines.

(John 3: 29b-30 MSG)

Are you familiar with the story of David and Jonathan from the Bible? The story can be found in 1 Samuel 16-18. Jonathan was the son of King Saul and heir to the kingdom. David was a shepherd boy, the youngest in his family, who had been responsible for taking care of the sheep and protecting them against wild animals. While in this role, unbeknownst to him, God was preparing David for the future battle he would face against the Philistine giant Goliath.

The whole Israelite army was afraid of Goliath, but one day when David was delivering cheese and bread to the soldiers, he heard Goliath's threats against their God. David, even though he was just a boy, was a man after God's own heart. When he heard the defiance, David asked, *Who is this uncircumcised Philistine that he should defy the armies of the living God?* (1 Samuel 17:17-26) I love the visual I get when I read that. I see David's passion that rises up inside of him. His defense was not from a place of pride but would stand against anyone who came against his God. In his righteous anger, David told King Saul that he would fight Goliath, arguing that the Lord would deliver him from the hand of the Philistine as he had with the lions and bears that threatened his herd.

Before David went off to battle, Saul dressed him in his armor, but the armor was not made for him. David took it off and went back to what he knew. Taking his staff and choosing five stones from the stream, David put them in his shepherd's pouch and, with his sling in hand, went to battle. He put one stone in his sling, struck Goliath, and killed him in one fell swoop just as he had done before with the lions and bears. (1 Samuel 17:31-51)

This is a valuable reminder we can take from David. Many times, as Christians, we become distracted by thoughts that we aren't good enough for the job. While what we have to offer may not look like much in our own eyes or even in the eyes of others, God has prepared us for what He asks of us.

When David returned from battle with the head of the enemy, Jonathan, heir of the king, became one in spirit with David. Instead of seeing a simple shepherd boy, Jonathan called out the king he saw in David. So much so that he made a covenant with him. In 1 Samuel 18:4, it says, *Jonathan took off the robe he was wearing and gave it to David, along with his tunic, and even his sword, his bow and belt.* It was the promise of his loving friendship.

Whether Jonathan knew at this moment that he would eventually hand over the kingdom is left to question, but it certainly makes for a beautiful representation, doesn't it? What is not in question is the love Jonathan had for David, which would ultimately bring him to surrender his kingship to the one God had chosen.

And Saul's son Jonathan went to David at Horesh and helped him find strength in God. "Don't be afraid," he said. "My father will not lay a hand on you. You will be king over Israel, and I will be second to you. Even my father Saul knows this."

(1 Samuel 23:16-17)

BE A JONATHAN

A friend of mine once told me I was her Jonathan. Many people may have taken it as a compliment, but I didn't want to be Jonathan. I took offense to the comment because I didn't want to *always* be labeled as "just" someone else's helper. Feeling resentful, I thought, *Go ahead and take the lead role. I will just hide here in the shadows.* I cried for days, hurt and even angry. I wanted to be David. And just like that—pride crept in. I allowed the enemy to distort something that was beautiful and twist the truth until all the beauty was squeezed out.

The truth was, I related with David on many levels throughout scripture. For example, we were both the youngest in our families. Some scholars even believe David may have struggled with depression, so we (David and I) had that in common as well. Like David, I also struggle with the sinfulness of my own flesh like he did while he was King of Israel. I have committed so many wrongs in my life, but the posture of my heart—no matter what—has always returned to a position of surrender and honor. I have been stubborn, bringing destruction in my life and the lives of others before I have a turn of heart. I don't take credit for the turn; this is the will of the Holy Spirit within me. Without Jesus, I am filthy rags, and left to my own, I will always make self-serving decisions.

I could have stayed in my pain and resentment and believed the lie that I was not important enough or good enough to be David, but even when I was full of my flesh, God lovingly revealed the truth as He sifted out the lies. Many times, this comes from my journaled conversations with God. For me, it's harder to write out the lies than it is to believe them in my mind. When I admit the lies, they become very real.

> *Lord,*
>
> *Please forgive me for feeling forgotten.*
>
> *I would see people, people that I have prayed with, even my own friends—things would be happening in their lives. Things we had prayed about together being answered, and at first I was jealous of their answered prayers, but you have helped me with that over the years so we were able to get past the jealousy, but it deceivingly turned into envy. I was happy for them but what about me God? What about my prayers? All the amazingly great things you have put on my heart, why are they there if they are never going to happen? Why have you forgotten me? It's not God, obviously, because he's still doing things all over the place—it must be me—of course! I'm not as disciplined, not as smart, not as capable, not as good of a time manager.* (Do you see the enemy's deception coming out in the previous sentence?)
>
> *But then God made me aware that nothing has changed on His end. He is faithful. What if He hasn't forgotten me, but I had forgotten Him? James 1:22-25: "Do not merely listen to the word and so deceive yourselves. Do what it says! Anyone who listens to the word but does not do what it says is like a man who looks at his face in a mirror and, after looking at himself, goes away and immediately forgets what he looks like. But the man who looks intently into the perfect law that gives freedom, and continues to do this, not forgetting what he has heard, but doing it, he will be blessed in what he does."*
>
> *2 Corinthians 3:16-18: "But whenever anyone turns to the Lord, the veil is taken away. Now the Lord is the Spirit, and where the Spirit of the*

Lord is, there is freedom. And we who with unveiled faces all reflect the Lord's glory, are being transformed into his likeness with ever increasing glory, which comes from the Lord, who is the Spirit."

During all of this I felt God ask me, "What if you are never a David and you are always a Jonathan?" I was heartbroken at the thought, God—I'm pretty sure you called me to be a David. What about all the dreams you've put on my heart? Immediately, the story of the rich young man in Mark 10:17-29 came to my mind. "If you want to be perfect go and sell your possessions and give to the poor, and you will have treasure in heaven. Then come, follow me. When the young man heard this he went away sad, because he had great wealth." (Mark 10:29) I humbled myself before God, and I said I do not want to be like him. Whatever You have for me, I will do. I am willing to be Jonathan. Help me to die to self and live for you. It's not about the qualities that I bring to the table, it is only dependent on my obedience.

From my time with God, I humbled myself before Him and surrendered my desires for His will. "God, if this is what you are calling me to, a life of servanthood, I surrender and I will obey. If you are calling me to a supporting role or, as much as it pains me to say, even backstage behind the curtains, with no light to be shed on my face, then God, I want to align with your will, and I trust you with my life."

I didn't realize the depth of character Jonathan must have had. He surrendered to the will of God, readily giving his legacy to David. It must have taken much humility and reverence. Did you know that Jonathan also had an armor bearer who stood behind him, ready to follow him into battle, who remained nameless? Let's just think about that for a moment. There are so many helpers throughout the Bible if we will open our eyes to see them. Sometimes they are the names we skim over, but we must be careful not to do this, because God's purpose prevails through all willing and obedient vessels.

TEAM WORK

I'm a basketball fan. I don't always know what's going on, but sitting in the stands, watching the fast-paced game and hearing the excited roar of the cheering crowd around me, is exhilarating. There's absolutely nothing like experiencing a team's camaraderie, especially one that has played together for years, witnessing how intricately they work together and perform like a well-oiled machine. They know each other's thoughts and prepare accordingly for the next move. You can feel the energy in the air. The unity is electric and thrilling!

When you're new to the game, it's easy to get infatuated with the standouts who are dunking, sinking impossible shots from behind the three-point line, or making insane blocks out of nowhere. These are sure to inspire the team and stir fires of excitement in the crowd. But I really appreciate it when a team's points are so evenly divided between its players that if the other team isn't careful and extremely attentive, the score will quickly get away from them and leave them unable to close the gap.

Players on teams like this are confident in their own ability to score but are equally confident in their team. So if they see another player who is lined up with a better position, they pass the ball to their teammate who scores and also get an assist on the record for themselves. On a team, all players matter. It's the same for us as the body of Christ. We are called to be a team that functions in unity. We have to be able to play well with others. Think of it like this: passing the ball is like planting a seed. Scoring the point is like watering the seed, and the win comes from God when He brings growth!

Paul states, *I planted the seed in your hearts, and Apollos watered it, but it was God who made it grow. It's not important who does the planting, or who does the watering. What's important is that God makes the seed grow. The one who plants and the one who waters work together with the same purpose. And both will be rewarded for their own hard work. For we are both God's workers. And you are God's field. You are God's building.* (1 Corinthians 3:6-9 NLT)

YOUR ROLE MATTERS

I've always wondered if Moses would have accomplished what he did without God giving him Aaron to speak on his behalf. (Exodus 4:14-16) Or if Joshua would have conquered the Amalekites if Moses wouldn't have led by example in his faith by holding his hands up in dependance on God during the battle? Or if Aaron and Hur weren't there to steady Moses's hands when he grew tired, would Joshua have walked away in defeat? (Exodus 17:10-16) This story has multiple characters who impacted the outcome by their obedience. We have to understand that to truly accomplish the will of God, we have to work together. Every single role is important to the body of Christ, and we need to function in our designated roles and not reach for the giftings of others.

So Joshua fought the Amalekites as Moses had ordered, and Moses, Aaron and Hur went to the top of the hill. As long as Moses held up his hands, the Israelites were winning, but whenever he lowered his hands, the Amalekites were winning. When Moses' hands grew tired, they took a stone and put it under him and he sat on it. Aaron and Hur held his hands up—one on one side, one on the other—so that his hands remained steady till sunset. So Joshua overcame the Amalekite army with the sword.

(Exodus 17:10-13)

SOWING AND REAPING

Henry Ford once said, "Whether you think you can or think you cannot, you are right." His quote gave me pause. Don't you wish all our negative sowing would just reap nothing? But that isn't the way the natural law of sowing and reaping works. Gotquestions.org explains it well: "We reap in kind to what we sow. Those who plant apple tree seeds should expect to harvest apples. Those who sow anger should expect to receive what anger naturally produces."

No matter how unimportant we may think our role is, we are still not exempt from the natural law of sowing and reaping. What if you are whole, you've just been sowing distorted seeds?

My friends, this can't go on. A spring doesn't gush fresh water one day and brackish the next, does it? Apple trees don't bear strawberries, do they? Raspberry bushes don't bear apples, do they? You're not going to dip into a polluted mud hole and get a cup of clear, cool water, are you?
(James 3:10-12 MSG)

When we sow seeds with our words and our actions, we choose what we plant and invest into our future. Sometimes it is helpful to ask ourselves, "What does that investment look like?" In five years, if we continue to do and say what we do today, will we be closer to what we want our lives and relationships to look like . . . or further away? So what we plant will grow and bear fruit, and it will be the fruit of which we eat. We are going to have a harvest of something, but what will it be? Will it be fruit that lasts?

THE PROMISE LAID OUT

I have sown into many false beliefs. For example, I've believed the lies that I am not good enough, that God isn't big enough, and my dreams are unreachable. But planting lies will only reap shame, bitterness, and hopelessness. We see this play out with the Israelites when God told Moses to pick twelve men from each tribe (representing the twelve tribes of Israel) to spy on the land of Canaan *that God was giving them.* (Numbers 13:1) However, it all went wrong when they returned and gave a report of what they saw. (Numbers 13:26-33)

Why do you think Moses said, *the land God was giving them?* Well, first of all, because God said it to him. Right? But there are other supporting reasons Moses was able to confidently proclaim that God was giving them the land. How about the encounter at the burning bush where God commissioned Moses? This promise was not new; it was the promise that drove the whole mission to exit Egypt, by way of the Red Sea.

God told Moses, *I am the God of your Father, the God of Abraham, Isaac, and Jacob. I've seen the misery of my people and I have come to rescue them and bring them to a land flowing with milk and honey and He proceeded to tell Moses, the home of the Canaanites, Hittites, Amorites, Perizzites, Hivites, and Jebusites.* (Exodus 3:6-10) But what would this have meant to Moses then? This commission didn't simply come out of thin air and fall on deaf ears. Because there was generational history, Moses would have known the promise God gave Abraham. So, let's rewind four hundred years and go all the way back to Abraham, Isaac, and Jacob (also known as Israel) to see what the full story is telling.

While Abram (before God changed his name to Abraham) lived in the land of Canaan, God told him he was giving him the land, north and south, east and west as far as he could see to him and his offspring forever. (Genesis 13:14-18) Then, God went on to tell Abram that his descendants would be enslaved for four hundred years but would come back to this same spot to take the land God was giving them. Now here they are three generations later, and everything seems to be falling into place in the fourth generation, as it is recorded in Genesis 15:16:

In the fourth generation your descendants will come back here, for the sin of the Amorites has not yet reached its full measure.

Here, we begin to put together that the twelve men Moses picked were the grandchildren of Israel, formerly known as Jacob. This means they were the great-great-grandchildren of Abraham. Think of the stories that have trickled down in your family and then remember this was a time when stories were the primary form of communication, told by grandparents to grandchildren and great-grandchildren. The stories of God's promised land had been passed down for several generations. The land God promised to Abraham and the land God told Moses would be flowing with milk and honey is the same land they are going to spy on. This is the land people! I have to believe that God sent them here first as a reminder of the covenant promise for their lineage, which would have meant something to them. But sometimes, even when there's very detailed history, including timelines and geographical locations to back up the promise, we can be so far removed that we begin to question its validity. I have to say, four hundred years is a long time to hold on to a promise.

PROMISES TO JOSHUA

So let's make another connection. It wasn't by accident that Joshua was one of the twelve spies sent out. Why do you think he was chosen? Well, let's break this down. The Bible tells us that they are in Canaan and about to go up through the Negev. (Numbers 13:17) But for us to understand the full importance of the scriptures, we have to know the relationship these people and places have with the Israelites. Who lived in the Negev? And what would this have meant to Joshua? The answer to these questions is found just a few verses later.

The Amalekites live in the Negev, the Hittites, Jebusites and Amorites
live in the hill country; and the Canaanites live near the sea and along the
Jordan river."
(Numbers 13: 29)

Amalekites? Wait, that name sounds familiar. Remember the battle mentioned earlier? The Amalekites were defeated when Aaron and Hur held Moses's hands up while Joshua fought. The Amalekites are the same people that Joshua defeated in battle. Isn't that so cool? Here's what happened next:

The Lord said to Moses, "Write this on a scroll as something to be
remembered and make sure that Joshua hears it, because I will
completely blot out the memory of Amalek under heaven."
(Exodus 17:14)

God reaffirmed His Word, that He defeated the Amalekites once before and he would do it again. God's gracious reminder was not only a generational promise but also a personal promise for the Israelites to write down so they would not forget. This promise was something tangible they could hold on to. Do you see how the story was built upon over the years? Every Israelite had historical proof to back up the promises of God. They had the promise that was given to their ancestors. Moses had firsthand experience at the burning bush. The Israelites had personal encounters of God's deliverance at the Red Sea and God's providence with water, manna, and quail that sustained them in the desert. God gave them victory over their enemies. And if that wasn't enough proof, directly before they are sent to spy on the land, Moses specifically tells them once more (for good measure) that God was giving it to them.

The twelve men explored the land God said would be a land flowing with milk and honey. The countryside brimmed with great fruitfulness, including large clusters of grapes richly saturated in the color purple, juicy pomegranates, and plump figs. However, their focus was redirected by the strikingly large men they also saw. In an instant, their faith in the promise turned into fear of men. When they gave the report, they all sowed seeds into the wrong jar, except for Caleb and Joshua. (Numbers 13:26-33) Even though the Promised Land was delivered into their hands, ripe for the taking, they forfeited their God-given right because of fear. (Numbers 13-14) They were promised the land, but they didn't believe God for the promise. They sowed words of destruction and death, and that is exactly what they got.

How long will this wicked community grumble against me? I have heard the complaints of these grumbling Israelites. So tell them, 'As surely as I live, declares the Lord, I will do to you the very things I heard you say: In this desert your bodies will fall—every one of you twenty years old or more who was counted in the census and who has grumbled against me. Not one of you will enter the land I swore with an uplifted hand to make your home, except Caleb son of Jephunneh and Joshua son of Nun. As for your children that you said would be taken for plunder, I will bring them in to enjoy the land you rejected.

(Numbers 14:27-31)

I get it though. They were completely human just like us. I am certainly guilty of complaining and doubting as well and asking for God's forgiveness, even in this moment. It's easy to look at the Israelites, who saw God's promises before them, and cast judgment. But what promises have *we* forgotten or forfeited for the instantaneous gratification of our flesh?

FACING YOUR GIANTS

If we believe in Jesus, we are also heirs to the promise. (Galatians 3:29) Our lives can be paralleled with the Israelites. I believe in every life, there is a history of God's providence to be found. What will our experience with His truth be? Just like David and the Israelites, we all have giants we will face, but we also have fruitful promises laid before us. Will we choose to remember all of God's rescue and glory from the past, holding tight to His unending faithfulness? Or will we allow the wilderness to fog our judgment, embitter our hearts, lengthen our suffering, and steal our promise?

The promise is ours for the taking, but it is contingent on our belief in God's promises and our response to God's unconditional love that never ceases to let us go. God is faithful. Will we be? I don't want to waste my time grumbling and complaining, stuck in desert situations because of my wavering faith.

I want to be like Caleb and Joshua, someone who sows into God's promises and not only into what our eyes can see. Will we remember His faithfulness? Will we show gratitude? Will we honor and obey? Will we believe? Will we remain faithful? Or will we reap a different outcome by what we choose to sow into? I hope we can glean from the Israelites' mistakes and not continue making the same ones ourselves. I pray for a repentant heart and a godly sorrow to reposition our perspective. God has already given us the promise of freedom. I encourage you to walk in Godly confidence and not regress in fear to the comfort of captivity.

One of the greatest compliments I have ever been given was from a friend repeating what another person said to her about me. "She makes me feel like a giant, like I could accomplish anything." The weight of this single comment, totaling a minuscule twelve words, hit me in a way I can't explain. The truth of the matter is I had no idea. I was just having coffee with a friend, encouraging and being encouraged, and this was the accolade I received. At just the right time, God shows us our importance in everyday moments.

Do not despise these small beginnings, for the Lord rejoices to see the work begin, to see the plumb line in Zerubbabel's hand.
(Zechariah 4:10 NLT)

Instead of viewing our enemies as giants, let's put them in the correct proportion to our Father and His authority over all. Let us speak life into those around us so they feel like giants through the Lord and they can stand firmly on His promises. May we be a people who remember his faithfulness and encourage others to do the same. So maybe it wasn't so bad being a Jonathan after all.

YOUR PURPOSE

We question over and over: What is my purpose? The answer is simple. My purpose and your purpose on this earth is to be restored to Christ and to point other people to Christ. Your purpose isn't found in a title or in works. It's only found in relationships: a relationship that comes from the Father, a relationship with the living Word, and a relationship with the Holy Spirit that overflows into the physical relationships God has brought into your life.

As God's fellow workers, we need to constantly remind ourselves that we are on the winning team. We are His ambassadors on a mission, carrying the torch each place we go. We are His help here on earth to fulfill His will to ensure every ear hears the good news.

All this is from God, who reconciled us to himself through Christ and gave us the ministry of reconciliation: that God was reconciling the

world to himself in Christ, not counting men's sins against them. And he
has committed to us the message of reconciliation. We are therefore
Christ's ambassadors, as though God were making his appeal through
us. We implore you on Christ's behalf: be reconciled to God.
(2 Corinthians 5:18-20)

YOUR FOCUS

A few weeks prior to writing this chapter, I got to hear Havilah Cunnington speak at the Beautiful Conference Women's Event held by Pearl Church in Denver, Colorado. She was speaking on the event of Peter walking on water in Matthew 14:29. She said she didn't believe the point of the story was the ability to walk on water or we would see many others doing this. The point was when Peter kept his focus on Jesus, the events around him didn't overtake him. If we did nothing else but seek God's face, we would get it right. If we would be willing to throw out every other agenda, we would be free to follow His. The Bible tells us we are unable to get it perfect on our own but in Jesus we can hold onto His promise.

In the end, when we've drawn our last our last breath, what will the people who love us most remember about us? Will it be our greatest successes or failures, our looks, our fashion, the job titles we held? Not at all. They will remember us for our character, our love, our encouragement, and the way we made them feel. *May we be like Jesus for this very reason. May we be the reason another believes upon the Lord. What better gift than an example of faith and the love of Christ. May we be steadfast in our faith. May we love like Jesus, forgive like Jesus, and be patient like Jesus.*

It is my deepest desire to know God's truth, believing His Word and sowing it into my own life and the lives of others. I want to walk upright—not perfectly but humbly. Be satisfied and grateful. Give grace like Jesus and have sincere joy. I pray I make a difference with the days I'm granted on this earth. I am beginning to understand the way to do this is one intentional moment at a time. Not seeking perfection or behavior modification but seeking the face of God.

May it be our heart's desire to seek His face in such a way that we can't help but be a reflection of the Lord so when others look at us, the only thing they see is Jesus. And we can be content looking like another face in the crowd. Even though Jesus has never viewed us that way.

Now we see but a poor reflection as in a mirror; then we shall see face to face. Now I know in part; then I shall know fully, even as I am fully known. And now these three remain: faith, hope and love. But the greatest of these is love.

(1 Corinthians 13:12-13)

Take a moment to pray and ask God if there are any promises you have forgotten.

In what way has God equipped you for your calling?

____

____

____

Who are the people God has placed in your life to be a team with, to practice unity?

____

____

____

Considering the law of sowing and reaping, if nothing changed in your life, what would you have to show for it?

____

____

____

What do you want your life to look like in three years? What can you work on in the sowing department to accomplish your desires?

____

____

____

HEALING IS ON THE HORIZON. I have created space for you to journal what stands out to you through your story. Please don't skip this step, as I believe it is where we release things we didn't even know we were holding on to. Write something—anything. Healing is coming!

SONG INSPIRATION

"Wild For Me" by Brandon Lake; "Trust in God" (feat. Chris Brown) LIVE by Elevation Worship; "Fear Is Not My Future" (feat. Brandon Lake & Chandler Moore) by Maverick City

Bibliography

Chapter 1

Ardolino, Emile, dir. *Dirty Dancing*. Chicago: Vestron Pictures, 1987.

Marshall, Garry, dir. *Pretty Woman*. Burbank: Buena Vista Pictures, 1990.

Chapter 2

Covey, Stephen R. *How to Develop Your Personal Mission Statement*. Grand Haven, MI: Grand Harbor Press, 2013.

Rice, Helen Steiner. *The Poems and Prayers of Helen Steiner Rice*. Ada, MI: Fleming H Revell Co., October 1, 2004.

Chapter 3

Merriam-Webster, s.v. "perfectionist (*n.*)," accessed October 8, 2023, https://www.merriam-webster.com/dictionary/perfectionist.

Meyer, Joyce. *Battlefield of the Mind: Winning the Battle in Your Mind*. New York: FaithWords, 2002.

Microsoft Bing, s.v. "disciple (*n.*)," accessed October 8, 2023, https://www.bing.com/search?q=disciple.

Warren, Rick. *The Purpose-Driven Life: What on Earth Am I Here For?* Grand Rapids, MI: Zondervan, 2002.

Chapter 4

Brown, Brené, *Daring Greatly: How the Courage to be Vulnerable Transforms the Way We Live, Love, Parent, and Lead.* New York: Avery, 2012.
"Joy comes to us in ordinary moments. We risk missing out when we get too busy chasing down the extraordinary."

Hancock, John Lee, dir. *The Blind Side.* Burbank: Warner Bros., 2009.

Chapter 5

Avildsen, John G., dir. *The Karate Kid.* Los Angeles: Columbia Pictures, 1984.
"If you only do what is easy, you will always remain weak."

Robbins, Mel. "The 5 Second Rule," Positive HiT, August 3, 2020. https://www.youtube.com/watch?v=2n41e9su3fM.

Robbins, Mel. *Stop Saying You're Fine: The No-BS Guide to Getting What You Want.* New York: Harmony/Rodale, 2012.
"That's what it takes to get what you want. Not big scary leaps once a year. It takes small, but irritating moves every single day."

Chapter 6

Bible App: https://www.bible.com/app.

Dictionary.com, s.v. "develop (*v.*)," accessed October 8, 2023, https://www.dictionary.com/browse/develop.

Dictionary.com, s.v. "discipline (*n.*)," accessed October 8, 2023, https://www.dictionary.com/browse/discipline.

Legrand, Louis. *The Tale of Two Wolves.* North Charleston, SC: CreateSpace, 2017.

Maxwell, John C. *The 15 Invaluable Laws of Growth: Live Them and Reach Your Potential.* New York: Center Street, 2014.
"Small disciplines repeated with consistency every day lead to great achievements gained slowly over time."

Smedes, Lewis B. *Forgive and Forget: Healing the Hurts We Don't Deserve.* San Francisco: HarperOne, 2007.
"To forgive is to set a prisoner free and discover that the prisoner was you."

Chapter 7
Luketic, Robert, dir. *Legally Blonde.* Beverly Hills: Metro-Goldwyn-Mayer Distributing Corporation (MGM), 2001.

Wood, Douglas. *The Secret of Saying Thanks.* New York: Simon & Schuster Books for Young Readers, 2005.
"The heart that gives thanks is a happy one, for we cannot feel thankful and unhappy at the same time."

Chapter 9
Graham, Billy. *Quotes from Billy Graham: A Legacy of Faith.* Brentwood, TN: B&H Publishing, 2013.
"Mountaintops are for views and inspiration, but fruit is grown in the valleys."

Chapter 10
Bible Reasons. "Bible Verses about Flowers." Accessed October 8, 2023. https://biblereasons.com/flowers/.
"God writes the gospel not in the Bible alone, but on trees and wildflowers and clouds and stars." —Martin Luther

Gaultiere, Bill. Soul Shepherding. "God's Wildflower." Accessed October 8, 2023. https://www.soulshepherding.org/gods-wildflower/.

GotQuestions.org. "What does the Bible say about coincidence?" Accessed October 8, 2023. https://www.gotquestions.org/Bible-coincidence.html.

Watchtower Online Library. "Are They Wildflowers or Weeds?" Accessed October 8, 2023. https://wol.jw.org/en/wol/d/r1/lp-e/102005408.

Chapter 12

Ford, Henry. GoodReads. Accessed October 8, 2023.
https://www.goodreads.com/quotes/978-whether-you-think-you-can-or-you-think-you-can-t--you-re.
"Whether you think you can or think you cannot, you are right."

GotQuestions.org. "What Does the Bible Say about Sowing and Reaping?" Accessed October 8, 2023. https://www.gotquestions.org/sowing-and-reaping.html.
"We reap in kind to what we sow. Those who plant apple tree seeds should expect to harvest apples. Those who sow anger should expect to receive what anger naturally produces."

Acknowledgments

I simply must give honor and gratitude to all the hands who have helped make this book possible. They say it takes a village to raise a child—I'd say the same for writing a book!

Havilah Cunnington and team for coming up with A Crash Course to Writing a Book, which broke down a huge mountain to climb into manageable molehills.

Jamie Glawson, a local author of *Faith, Trust and Pixie Dust*, for being willing to share her experience and contacts with me over coffee.

Janelle Keith, my writing coach, for surprisingly turning my single run-on sentence into a book.

Lori Clapper, Woven Books developmental editor, for her amazing editing skills.

Kim Bookless, copyeditor and proofreader, for bringing excellence to the manuscript's final details.

Bethany Brown, owner of The Cadence Group, who worked diligently to pull it all together and get me to the finish line.

Gwyn, owner of GKS Creative, for turning my book into a wonderfully beautiful package inside and out.

May God bless you all!

About the Author

AMY BRIDGES lives in Beaumont, Texas, a small town on the map between Houston and the Texas/Louisiana state border. She has been married for twenty-three years and is a mom to three adult children, two biological and one bonus child. These people are her life. She has a love for birds, trees, and talking with friends over coffee about deep matters of the heart. Her favorite adventures are flying with her husband and traveling. She's down to earth and thrives on authenticity. If she is home, you can bet she's removed *all clothing with wire* and found some comfy pajamas to change into. Now that she loves life, her goal is to keep loving life, encourage women to never give up, and help them process their struggles to find life was meant to be enjoyed.